Workless

Workless

Matthew Petchinsky

Workless: Escape the 9-5 Without Being Broke

By: Matthew Petchinsky

Disclaimer

This book is a creative and educational exploration of alternative lifestyles, income strategies, and mindset shifts designed to help readers live with greater freedom and intention. It is **not financial, legal, or employment advice**. Readers should always consult qualified professionals before making major financial, business, or career decisions.

The author's perspectives are based on personal insights, research, and real-world examples meant to inspire self-reliance and critical thinking—not to replace individualized professional guidance. The results discussed are not guaranteed and will vary depending on personal circumstances, effort, and context.

By reading this book, you acknowledge that the author and publisher are **not responsible for any financial outcomes, employment changes, or life decisions** made based on its contents. This work is intended as a **motivational and informational guide** for those seeking new ways to thrive beyond traditional employment systems.

Introduction: Breaking the Work = Worth Illusion

For over a century, we've been trained to equate *working hard* with *being worthy*. The modern world tells us our value is measured by our productivity, our job title, or the digits on our paystub. "Busy" has become a badge of honor, exhaustion a status symbol. We sacrifice our health, relationships, and inner peace at the altar of the 9-to-5—often for jobs that drain us more than they sustain us.

But what if this equation was never real? What if "work = worth" was the illusion that keeps modern economies humming—and most people trapped?

Workless: Escape the 9-5 Without Being Broke is a blueprint for dismantling that illusion, step by step. It's not about laziness or rebellion for rebellion's sake—it's about designing a system where your time, energy, and dignity belong to *you*. This book teaches how to downshift your life intelligently, reduce financial pressure without reducing quality of life, and navigate society's invisible rules to your advantage.

The truth is, the 9-5 model was designed for a world that no longer exists. The Industrial Age needed predictable workers; the Digital Age rewards adaptable creators. Yet most of us are still operating under the same assumptions our grandparents lived by—work for decades, retire when you're too tired to enjoy it, and hope it was all worth it. But in today's world, automation replaces jobs faster than education systems can adapt, corporations drain human attention for profit, and burnout has become the default state of adulthood.

The time has come to reclaim our autonomy—not just financially, but spiritually and psychologically. This is not about quitting your job tomorrow. It's about engineering a life where you *could*—and still thrive.

In these pages, you'll learn how to:

- Identify and dismantle internalized beliefs that link self-worth to output.
- Redefine "success" around freedom, not just finances.
- Build sustainable income systems that don't require constant presence.
- Design a minimalist but meaningful lifestyle that amplifies joy instead of consumption.
- Navigate the emotional detox that comes from leaving the societal treadmill.

To live "workless" is not to live idle—it is to live *intentional*. It's choosing impact over image, balance over burnout, and self-determination over blind obedience. This book will teach you to spot the loopholes in modern systems—economic, digital, and social—and to use them not for exploitation, but liberation.

Every generation inherits myths. Ours inherited the myth of endless productivity. This book exists to dismantle it—and to show that a life of purpose, dignity, and independence doesn't require endless labor. It only requires courage, clarity, and a willingness to design your own reality.

Welcome to *Workless*. You're not escaping work—you're escaping **wage dependency** disguised as purpose.

Now, let's begin redesigning your life—one liberated choice at a time.

Chapter 1: Redefining Wealth as Time

For most people, wealth has always meant money—bank balances, assets, and the ability to purchase comfort. Yet true wealth is far older, simpler, and far more personal. It's the one currency every living being shares, and yet it's the only one we can never replenish: **time**.

This chapter invites you to challenge one of the deepest societal myths—that wealth is measured in dollars, possessions, or professional prestige—and to replace it with a model where **time itself becomes the ultimate measure of freedom**.

The Illusion of Monetary Wealth

From an early age, we are taught that time is something to be *spent* to earn money. "Time is money," they say. But in truth, money is just a tool to *buy back* time—if we use it wisely. The tragedy of modern society is that most people spend their healthiest years trading away time for the promise of freedom later. By the time retirement arrives, health, curiosity, and vitality have already been drained by decades of overwork.

The system works only if people keep believing that money is scarce and time is expendable. Corporations rely on this belief. The "work = worth" illusion convinces us that being constantly busy makes us valuable. But busyness is not value—it's *distraction*. It keeps us from asking the question that terrifies the system most: **What if I stopped playing this game altogether?**

Time as the True Currency

When you begin seeing time as your most precious asset, every decision shifts. Suddenly, you start asking:

- How much *time freedom* will this purchase or commitment cost me?
- Am I buying a life of maintenance or a life of meaning?
- Do I own my hours, or have I sold them?

Time wealth is measured not by how much you can buy, but by how freely you can live. It's the ability to wake up without dread, to pursue creativity or rest without guilt, to eat slowly, think deeply, and experience your life while you're living it.

Someone making $30,000 a year but controlling their entire schedule might be wealthier than someone making $300,000 who never sees the sun. Wealth, in this new model, is not *accumulation*. It's **autonomy**.

The Hidden Costs of False Wealth

Every extra possession demands maintenance. Every upgrade comes with new expectations. The chase for more keeps you tethered to jobs you hate, screens that drain you, and a version of success that no longer fits. True wealth, then, becomes an act of *subtraction*—removing everything that steals your hours without returning meaning.

When you redefine wealth as time, luxury becomes quiet mornings, creative afternoons, and the absence of hurry. You begin to measure prosperity in moments of peace, not possessions. You start seeing that "having enough" is not a limitation—it's liberation.

The Science of Time Freedom

Psychological research supports what minimalist and slow-living movements have known for decades: when people gain control of their time, their happiness rises dramatically. Studies show that those who spend money on time-saving services or flexible lifestyles report greater life satisfaction than those who spend on material goods. The conclusion is clear—**time autonomy directly correlates with emotional well-being**.

By designing a life that requires less, you gain more: more focus, more health, more meaning. "Workless" living is not about abandoning effort—it's about aligning effort with what genuinely matters.

Exercises in Reframing

To begin redefining wealth in your own life, start by observing how you use your hours. Track your week—not by productivity, but by *presence*. Where do your hours go? What drains you? What restores you? Once you identify the "time leaks" in your life—commutes, tasks that could be automated, social obligations that add no value—you can begin patching them one by one.

Remember: every reclaimed hour is wealth restored.

Journal Prompts: Redefining Wealth as Time

1. What does "wealth" mean to me right now—and how has that definition been influenced by family, school, or society?
2. When was the last time I felt truly rich in time, not money? What was I doing, and why did it feel that way?
3. If I measured success purely by peace, what would my life look like?
4. What daily activities feel like "time drains," and how could I reduce or eliminate them?
5. How much of my current spending supports time freedom versus time debt?
6. What would a "rich day" look like if money were irrelevant? Describe it in detail.
7. What emotions arise when I imagine having far more free time but earning less money?
8. Which responsibilities do I maintain out of fear or social expectation rather than genuine need?
9. How can I start trading money *for* time instead of time *for* money?
10. If I had only one year to live, what parts of my schedule would immediately vanish—and what would remain?

To redefine wealth as time is to rebel quietly against a system that profits from your exhaustion. Every small shift toward owning your hours—whether it's simplifying your needs, cutting unnecessary commitments, or reimagining your income—builds a new kind of wealth: one rooted in sovereignty, not servitude.

Because in the end, money is only paper until it buys back what truly matters—**your time, your freedom, and your life.**

Chapter 2: Micro-Exit Plans from Work Slavery

Freedom rarely begins with a dramatic leap; it begins with a quiet plan. Most people fantasize about walking out of their jobs in a blaze of defiance, but in reality, sustainable escape from what can only be called **work slavery**—the endless cycle of dependency, exhaustion, and fear—requires strategy, not rebellion. This chapter is your field manual for building those small, practical escape routes—**micro-exits**—that collectively dismantle the illusion of captivity one system at a time.

The Myth of the Big Leap

The corporate narrative wants you to believe there are only two options: stay trapped in the 9-5 or risk everything to "go freelance" overnight. Both extremes keep you scared. Fear maintains obedience. The truth is more nuanced: **you can leave gradually, intelligently, and safely**.

A micro-exit is any action that gives you more control over your time, money, or environment without requiring total upheaval. It's the art of quietly shifting leverage in your favor until you no longer need permission to live freely. Each micro-exit chips away at dependency, reducing the system's ability to dictate your choices.

Understanding Work Slavery

Work slavery is not just about physical labor—it's emotional and psychological. It's the chronic fear of unemployment, the dependence on a single paycheck, and the cultural shame attached to rest. It's being told your loyalty to a company defines your moral worth, even as that company replaces you the moment profits drop.

To break free, you must recognize that modern work systems are **attention extraction machines**. They harvest human focus the way industrial farms harvest crops—efficiently and without compassion. A micro-exit begins when you stop letting others define what your time is worth.

Building Micro-Exits: The Strategic Layers

Each micro-exit can be understood through five key layers of autonomy. You don't have to master all at once—start with one, and the rest follow naturally.

1. **Financial Autonomy:**
   Create one small income stream outside your employer. It can be digital products, tutoring, freelancing, reselling, or small-batch crafts. The goal isn't immediate riches; it's to prove to yourself that money can arrive *without* your boss. This psychological shift is the first real crack in the system.
2. **Skill Reallocation:**
   Every hour you spend outside work can either numb or empower you. Use it to learn tools that move you closer to independence—automation, marketing, minimalism, or new trades. The moment you stop being *only* what your employer trained you to be, you become unpredictable to the system—and therefore freer.
3. **Lifestyle Downshifting:**
   Reduce the overhead that keeps you chained. Move to a smaller place, sell unused subscriptions, and stop equating comfort with consumption. Every reduced bill is a micro-exit because it lowers the threshold of how much income you need to stay alive. Freedom isn't earned—it's *un-owed*.
4. **Time Reclamation:**
   Audit your hours like an accountant. If you spend eight hours at work and four recovering from it, you've lost half your waking life to servitude. Start reclaiming thirty minutes a day for self-driven projects. Those thirty minutes, protected fiercely, become the seed of sovereignty.
5. **Mental Deprogramming:**
   Society rewards exhaustion with praise. Begin rewiring this. Each time you rest without guilt, each time you say no to unpaid over-

time, you are staging a psychological micro-exit. Your mind must leave before your body can follow.

The Compounding Effect of Small Freedoms

Think of micro-exits as a portfolio of liberation. The first side income might earn $50 a month. Then $200. Then $1,000. The first boundary at work might reclaim one weekend, then every weekend. Over time, these small acts accumulate into a life that no longer depends on corporate permission slips.

What begins as a whisper becomes momentum. The goal is to design a reality where leaving your job becomes a **choice**, not a crisis. True wealth is not quitting; it's being able to quit *anytime you want.*

Micro-Exit Mindset Shifts

- **From Loyalty to Leverage:** You owe your employer labor, not life.
- **From Fear to Experimentation:** Treat freedom as an ongoing prototype, not a final destination.
- **From Escaping to Designing:** Don't run away from work—build toward autonomy.
- **From Debt to Ownership:** Every dollar you save or invest toward independence is a silent rebellion.
- **From Pleasing to Planning:** Stop trying to be the perfect employee; start being the competent architect of your escape.

These shifts reprogram the subconscious obedience that modern work culture thrives on. You can't free yourself from a system whose values you still believe in.

Case Study: The 15-Minute Revolution

One reader, Alicia, began her escape by setting a 15-minute timer each evening after her shift. During that time, she researched micro-business ideas, tracked her spending, and wrote down her emotional state. Within six months, she had created an online store that replaced 30% of her income. Within a year, she moved to part-time employment by choice.

Alicia's story is not exceptional—it's *replicable*. The difference between dreamers and escapees is consistency, not luck. Every person has 15 minutes that can be reallocated toward freedom.

Protecting Your Micro-Exit

The early stages are fragile. Doubt will arrive dressed as practicality. Friends will call you unrealistic. Employers will sense disengagement and try to re-entangle you with raises or recognition. Protect your micro-exit plan like an ember in the wind.

Journal your progress, visualize your end state, and remember: every small win matters. The system wants you distracted by scale; liberation happens through *small, deliberate defiance.*

Journal Prompts: Designing Your Micro-Exits

1. What aspects of my job feel most imprisoning—and what small actions could weaken their control?
2. What skills do I already have that could generate independent income within 30 days?
3. How could I simplify my lifestyle to reduce dependence on my paycheck by 10% this month?
4. What emotion stops me from imagining life outside traditional work—and where did it originate?
5. If I could free just one hour per day for myself, how would I use it to move closer to autonomy?
6. What does my ideal "micro-exit" look like six months from now? Be specific.
7. How can I transform rest and recovery into active resistance against overwork culture?
8. Which subscriptions, habits, or expenses currently own more of my life than they deserve?
9. How would I respond if offered more money to stay trapped—what boundaries must I set now?
10. What one micro-exit action can I commit to this week that proves freedom is already possible?

Each micro-exit is an act of quiet revolution. You don't need permission to leave; you only need a plan. By mastering these gradual exits, you rewire both your mind and your reality—proving that the power once outsourced to a paycheck has always belonged to you.

Chapter 3: Living on 50% Less Without Feeling Poor

The secret to escaping the 9-to-5 isn't earning more—it's needing less. Most people believe financial freedom is reserved for high earners or lucky investors, but true freedom often begins with **radical simplicity**. Learning to live on half of what you used to spend is not deprivation—it's transformation. It's the art of *designing sufficiency* instead of endlessly chasing excess.

This chapter teaches how to cut your expenses by 50% without shrinking your quality of life, your sense of dignity, or your children's joy. The goal isn't austerity—it's **abundance without dependency**.

The Psychological Trap of "Enough"

We live in a world engineered to make you feel perpetually behind. The marketing machine whispers that happiness lies just beyond the next purchase: the newer phone, the bigger home, the higher-tier subscription. This constant hunger fuels the work-spend-debt cycle that keeps people trapped.

But the truth is that "enough" isn't a number—it's a mindset. Once you decouple *worth* from *wealth*, you begin to realize that most expenses are not needs but narratives.

When you redefine what wealth looks like—quiet mornings, debt-free evenings, more family time, fewer financial fears—you begin to live richer on less.

The Math of Meaning: 50% Less, 100% More Freedom

Living on 50% less doesn't mean cutting your life in half—it means cutting **waste**, not joy. Most households can reclaim 30–60% of their spending through intentional design, not sacrifice.

Here's how:

1. **Audit Everything**
   Track every expense for 30 days. Highlight what truly contributes to well-being versus what simply fills time or maintains appearances. Most "necessities" vanish under honest observation.
2. **Simplify Housing**
   Housing is the biggest trap. Downsizing, relocating, or even house-sharing temporarily can free thousands per year. Smaller homes often create *more connection*, less clutter, and lower stress.
3. **Master Food Systems**
   Learn bulk cooking, freezing, and meal planning. One pot of soup, stew, or rice base can feed a family affordably without feeling repetitive. Teach kids to join meal prep—it becomes an education in sustainability and gratitude, not scarcity.
4. **Eliminate Subscription Creep**
   Cancel every automatic payment that doesn't directly contribute to education, health, or income. Streaming platforms and "small" monthly charges quietly drain power from your future self.
5. **Reimagine Transportation**
   Walk more, bike, or share rides. Selling a second car or switching to an older paid-off model can save thousands yearly without reducing life satisfaction—especially when the tradeoff is more time together.
6. **Choose Experiences Over Objects**
   Redirect spending toward memories, not merchandise. Free local adventures, community events, or creative family projects yield more fulfillment than constant consumer upgrades.

7. **Redefine Luxury**
   Luxury isn't designer goods—it's having an afternoon nap without guilt, eating a home-cooked meal with your kids, or taking a weekday off because you can.

Living on Less with Kids: Teaching Freedom Early

Children learn their relationship with money by observing yours. The best inheritance you can give them isn't wealth—it's wisdom.

- **Involve Them in Choices:**
  Frame simplicity as empowerment. "We're saving for adventures," not "We can't afford that." Teach them that conscious spending equals independence.
- **Turn Frugality into Fun:**
  Host "Zero-Spend Weekends" where the challenge is creativity, not consumption—build forts, explore parks, invent home games, cook together. Kids remember connection, not receipts.
- **Educate Early:**
  Show them the basics of saving, sharing, and earning. Give them small responsibilities—like budgeting a family outing or tracking grocery savings. It turns scarcity into strategy.
- **Prioritize Presence Over Presents:**
  Studies repeatedly show that children measure love in *time*, not *toys*. By freeing yourself from financial strain, you give them something priceless: *you.*

The Emotional Shift: From Consumer to Creator

Once you escape the reflex to buy every solution, you rediscover your own inventiveness. Making, repairing, repurposing—these are not signs of poverty; they are acts of creative wealth.

A minimalist mindset fosters deeper relationships, more gratitude, and less anxiety. You begin to see that abundance was never about ownership—it was about *energy*.

Every dollar not spent becomes stored freedom. Every item not bought becomes more mental space. And every simplified habit becomes a small act of rebellion against the lie that happiness is for sale.

Building a "Half-Cost Life" Without Half the Joy

You can live on 50% less while doubling your sense of security if you:

- Replace paid entertainment with shared creativity.
- Reduce energy usage through conscious scheduling (daylight work, unplugged evenings).
- Grow small portions of your food—even herbs or sprouts.
- Embrace barter, trade, or mutual-aid systems within your community.
- Repair before replacing—each fix strengthens self-reliance.

Over time, you'll notice a pattern: the less you depend on external consumption, the more *internal freedom* you feel. You are no longer surviving—you are designing.

Journal Prompts: Living Well on Less

1. What are the top five expenses in my life that do not genuinely contribute to happiness or health?
2. How would my definition of wealth change if my income were cut in half tomorrow?
3. What purchases do I make to impress others, and how could I replace them with authenticity?
4. How can I involve my children or family in the process of simplifying without them feeling deprived?
5. What experiences have given me deep joy that cost nothing or very little?
6. How could I transform "budgeting" from restriction into a creative challenge?
7. What emotional triggers lead me to spend unnecessarily, and what healthier responses could replace them?
8. How could I redesign my daily routine to waste less time, energy, or money?
9. What would a "rich" day look like if material possessions were irrelevant?
10. How can I measure my success by freedom, not finances, over the next six months?

Living on less is not failure—it's freedom disguised as simplicity. When you learn to thrive on 50% less, you reclaim the right to live on your own terms. You begin to experience life as it was meant to be lived—unrushed, uncluttered, and unburdened.

By the end of this process, you will realize something radical: **you were never poor. You were just paying too much for your own captivity.**

Chapter 4: Raising Free Children — Living Well on Less with Kids (Ages 0–18)

Living on less becomes more meaningful—not harder—when children are part of the journey. Each stage of childhood brings its own financial pressures and emotional nuances, but it also offers opportunities to teach resilience, creativity, and true wealth: freedom of thought, time, and self-worth.

This chapter walks you through how to design a fulfilling, minimalist lifestyle for families with children of all ages, from newborns to young adults. You'll learn how to reduce costs *without deprivation*, nurture independence, and raise kids who understand that a life well-lived is not measured by money, but by meaning.

The Core Philosophy: Love Over Luxury

Children don't need more—they need *you*.

What they crave most—presence, attention, laughter—costs nothing. The problem is that modern society conditions parents to compensate for absence with consumption. We buy toys, gadgets, trips, and distractions to replace what we can't give: unhurried time and calm energy.

When you begin to live on less, you start reclaiming both. Simplicity allows you to be emotionally available again. A smaller life doesn't make childhood smaller—it makes it **deeper**.

Infants and Toddlers (0–3 Years): The Minimalist Beginning

This is the stage where consumer marketing hits hardest. Parents are told they need every gadget, stroller, and sterilizer to be "good caregivers." In truth, babies thrive on consistency, not consumption.

How to Live on Less (Without Sacrificing Comfort):

- **Borrow, Don't Buy:** Babies outgrow gear within months. Borrow from friends or community parenting groups. Many neighborhoods have "baby swaps" for clothes and toys.
- **Skip the Designer Baby Myth:** Branding preys on parental guilt. Comfort, safety, and love are all that matter—not labels.
- **Focus on the Five Essentials:** Shelter, nourishment, hygiene, sleep, and love. Everything else is optional.
- **Homemade Baby Food:** Simple blended fruits, vegetables, and grains cost a fraction of store-bought options and are often healthier.
- **Routine Over Material:** Babies crave predictable rhythms, not expensive stimulation. A consistent nap, meal, and play schedule brings peace to both parent and child.

Freedom Lesson: Teach that love is not transactional. Babies absorb the energy of presence long before they understand possessions.

Preschoolers (4–6 Years): The Age of Imagination

At this stage, kids are sponges of creativity—and consumer culture knows it. You'll see endless pressure for brand-name clothes, theme-park birthdays, and "educational" devices. Yet, the richest learning experiences come from play, not purchases.

How to Live on Less (and Make It Magical):

- **Creative Play Zones:** Use recycled materials to build forts, castles, or craft projects. A cardboard box can entertain a child longer than a $200 toy.
- **Library Adventures:** Local libraries are goldmines for free books, storytimes, and kids' events.
- **Nature Schooling:** Walks in nature teach science, mindfulness, and gratitude—all for free.
- **Gift Alternatives:** Encourage relatives to give *experiences*, not toys—museum passes, nature kits, or family movie nights.
- **Zero-Spend Celebrations:** Birthdays don't need hired entertainers or themed venues. Homemade cupcakes, park games, and laughter create stronger memories.

Freedom Lesson: Show them that joy doesn't come from stores—it comes from stories, creativity, and imagination.

Early School Age (7–10 Years): The Awareness Stage

Children at this age begin comparing their lives to others. This is where the "feeling poor" narrative can creep in if not reframed early.

How to Live on Less Without Them Feeling Deprived:

- **Include Them in Decisions:** Be transparent about budgeting and saving goals. Let them see you prioritize what matters.
- **Gamify Frugality:** Turn cost-saving into a challenge—who can find the cheapest healthy lunch recipe or the best thrift-store treasure?
- **Encourage Mini-Earning Projects:** Lemonade stands, helping neighbors, or selling crafts instill independence and the value of resourcefulness.
- **Reframe Comparison:** Teach them that every family makes choices. Some choose more things; others choose more time together.
- **Focus on Identity, Not Image:** Praise curiosity, kindness, and creativity—not possessions.

Freedom Lesson: Teach that living differently isn't being "less than"—it's being *awake* in a world that's asleep.

Preteens (11–13 Years): The Age of Influence

As peers and media begin shaping identity, financial restraint can clash with the desire to "fit in." This is a pivotal age for teaching inner worth and conscious independence.

How to Live on Less (and Build Emotional Wealth):

- **Digital Detox Cycles:** Limit exposure to social media marketing that breeds envy and dissatisfaction.
- **Financial Transparency:** Share how consumer debt traps families. Understanding systems early builds rebellion against manipulation.
- **Empower Choice:** Give them a modest allowance with the responsibility to budget. Let mistakes happen—they're lessons, not failures.
- **DIY Identity:** Encourage self-expression through creativity, fashion upcycling, or crafts instead of constant consumption.
- **Model Confidence:** Speak positively about your lifestyle choices. Kids mirror your attitude—if you feel free, they'll feel proud, not deprived.

Freedom Lesson: Teach them to measure self-worth by contribution, not consumption.

Teenagers (14–18 Years): The Independence Apprenticeship

By now, the goal shifts from protection to preparation. Teen years are the bridge between dependency and autonomy. This is the stage where living on less transforms into *empowered living*.

How to Live on Less While Teaching Financial Mastery:

- **Part-Time Purpose:** Encourage entrepreneurial thinking—reselling, freelancing, tutoring, or digital creativity. Show them that money can be created ethically and independently.
- **Minimalist Tech:** Limit upgrades. A functional device is enough. Teach the cost of digital debt and planned obsolescence.
- **Teach Value Over Price:** Explain how every dollar saved buys future freedom—travel, education, or time off.
- **Budget as a Family:** Involve teens in grocery lists, energy savings, and big-picture decisions. When they understand costs, they develop gratitude instead of entitlement.
- **Dream Freedom, Not Debt:** Talk openly about student loans, credit cards, and lifestyle inflation. Help them design life goals around *freedom of time*, not lifelong obligation.

Freedom Lesson: Independence isn't about earning more—it's about *needing less* and choosing your own direction.

The Unified Family Vision

Living on less with kids is not about restriction—it's about **reconstruction**. You are rebuilding the family economy around connection, creativity, and consciousness.

When children grow up in this system, they carry forward unshakable lessons:

- Wealth is measured in time and trust.
- Happiness doesn't come from endless consumption.
- Freedom begins the moment you stop borrowing identity from a paycheck.

The result? Kids who don't fear simplicity, but embrace it. Kids who don't chase status, but create meaning. Kids who see that less can indeed be *limitless*.

Journal Prompts: Raising Free Children in a Simple World

1. What messages about money and "success" do I unconsciously model for my kids?
2. How can I replace material rewards with emotional or experiential ones?
3. What are three low-cost family traditions I could start this month?
4. How can I help my children understand the difference between "less" and "lack"?
5. What free or community resources could replace current paid activities?
6. How can I teach my children to participate in saving and simplifying without anxiety?
7. What does a "wealthy childhood" look like when measured in love and learning?
8. How can I prepare my teens for adult independence while keeping family connection strong?
9. What part of our family budget reflects fear rather than freedom?
10. How will our children describe our lifestyle when they grow up—stressed and busy, or simple and free?

Final Thought:

When you live on less with children, you're not limiting their future—you're expanding it. You're teaching them the art of sovereignty in a world addicted to servitude. You're raising a generation that doesn't measure life by what they earn, but by how fully they *live*.

Chapter 5: The Bill-Slayer's Blueprint — Mastering Water, Power, and Rent Freedom

Bills are modern chains disguised as necessities. Each one—water, electricity, rent—feels fixed, immovable, and non-negotiable. But in truth, these "essentials" can be dramatically reduced or restructured once you understand the hidden systems behind them. Most people lose hundreds, sometimes thousands, of dollars each year to waste, inefficiency, and outdated living patterns.

This chapter will teach you how to **cut your household bills by 30–70%** without sacrificing comfort, dignity, or health. The goal isn't to live in darkness or deprivation—it's to reclaim your **power (literally and financially)** by mastering every leak, drain, and loophole in your living system.

Section I: The Mindset Shift — From Consumer to Custodian

You are not a passive "user" of utilities—you are the manager of your personal ecosystem. Every dollar that leaves your household is a form of energy leaving your life. The sooner you view your home as a living organism—with energy inputs, water flows, and space utilization—the sooner you begin to master it.

Freedom begins with awareness:

- Every utility bill is a *map* of dependency.
- Every reduction is a *return* of autonomy.
- Every conservation habit is a *rebellion* against financial waste.

Once you stop assuming "it can't be helped," you open the door to innovation.

Part 1: Water — The Hidden Wealth You're Flushing Away

Water bills are sneaky—they seem small until you realize how easily they compound. A dripping faucet can waste up to 3,000 gallons a year. A leaky toilet? Over 25,000. You're literally paying to lose control of your resources.

Practical Water-Saving Systems

1. **Audit Your Flow:**
   Check every tap, pipe, and toilet for leaks. A $3 washer ring can save you hundreds per year.
2. **Low-Flow, High-Sense Fixtures:**
   Modern low-flow showerheads and faucet aerators reduce usage by up to 50% with no loss of comfort.
3. **The "One Flush Rule":**
   For households with children, teach that every unnecessary flush equals pennies lost.
   Use "if it's yellow, let it mellow" as a conscious (and sanitary) rule when appropriate.
4. **Shower Smarter:**
   Limit showers to 5 minutes. Make it a timed family challenge. Play one favorite song—when it ends, water off.
5. **Reuse and Reclaim:**
   - Collect shower warm-up water in a bucket for plants or cleaning.
   - Capture rainwater if local laws allow (many do, with limits).
6. **Laundry Liberation:**
   Wash only full loads and use cold water when possible. Cold cycles protect clothes, save money, and reduce energy waste from heating.

7. **Greywater Mindset:**
   Don't let clean water go down the drain when it could be reused for rinsing, soaking, or mopping.
8. **Landscaping Wisdom:**
   Replace grass lawns with native plants, rock gardens, or clover—these need less water and maintenance.

Result: A typical household can cut water bills by 40–60% without a single sacrifice in hygiene or comfort.

Part 2: Electricity — Rewiring the Modern Dependency

Electricity is both the most powerful and most easily abused utility. The modern home leaks power the way old roofs leak rain—quietly and constantly. Lights left on, idle devices, heating and cooling waste—it all drains both wallet and world.

Energy Autonomy Strategies

1. **Identify Phantom Loads:**
   Unplug chargers, game consoles, and small appliances when not in use. They drain power even when "off." Power strips with switches make this easy.
2. **Light Like a Minimalist:**
   - Switch to LED bulbs (they last up to 25x longer).
   - Use warm light in evenings to promote relaxation and save energy.
   - Try motion-sensor lights in hallways or bathrooms.
3. **Temperature Control = Bill Control:**
   - Set thermostats to 68°F in winter and 78°F in summer. Every degree outside that range adds 3–5% to your bill.
   - Use fans before A/C; wear layers before turning up heat.
   - Seal windows and doors—weatherstripping costs under $20 and saves hundreds yearly.
4. **Appliance Rotation:**
   Large appliances (dishwasher, dryer) are energy hogs. Use them off-peak—usually at night or weekends—to lower rates if your utility offers time-based pricing.
5. **Daylight Harvesting:**
   Rearrange furniture to maximize natural light. It's free, healthy, and dramatically cuts lighting needs.
6. **The Two-Hour Rule:**
   Limit unnecessary screen or entertainment device use. You're not just saving electricity—you're saving mental clarity.

7. **DIY Solar Starter:**
   Even a small portable solar panel (under $150) can charge devices and run lamps during outages or emergencies. It's a micro-step toward energy independence.
8. **Fridge and Freezer Optimization:**
   Keep them full (air gaps waste cooling). Clean coils every few months to improve efficiency.
9. **Water Heater Wisdom:**
   Lower the temperature to 120°F. It's safe, comfortable, and slashes costs.

Result: Combine these methods and you'll likely see **30–50% savings on electricity**—plus the psychological reward of knowing *you're no longer fully plugged into dependency.*

Part 3: Rent — The Silent Anchor

Rent is usually the largest expense, yet most people treat it as untouchable. But even here, creative solutions can drastically reduce cost—or eliminate it entirely. The key is to view housing not as a static bill, but as a negotiable *system of value exchange.*

Rent Reduction & Freedom Strategies

1. **Downsize Strategically:**
   Most families use only 40–60% of their space efficiently. Consider smaller units, shared housing, or co-living arrangements that still provide privacy but cut costs.
2. **Negotiate with Data:**
   Landlords respect informed tenants. Research comparable rentals nearby and use that data to request lower rent, longer leases, or included utilities.
3. **Offer Value Exchange:**
   Barter services like maintenance, painting, gardening, or digital marketing in exchange for partial rent reductions. Many landlords, especially private owners, are open to creative agreements.
4. **Relocate for Leverage:**
   Moving even 10–15 miles from high-cost areas can slash rent by 20–40%. Use remote work flexibility or hybrid options to your advantage.
5. **Shared Housing Renaissance:**
   Renting a multi-room house with trustworthy roommates or extended family can cut costs in half. Clear written agreements protect harmony.
6. **Subletting Smartly:**
   If your lease allows, rent out unused rooms or storage space. This creates passive rent offset.

7. **Long-Term Stability Agreements:**
   Offer to sign a longer lease in exchange for fixed rates—landlords value guaranteed occupancy over short-term gains.
8. **Seasonal Renting:**
   Negotiate lower rates during off-peak months. Many properties are discounted in winter or post-summer seasons.
9. **Micro-Housing & Tiny Living:**
   For those seeking independence, micro-apartments or tiny homes (purchased or built) reduce monthly expenses while maintaining ownership potential.
10. **Path to Ownership Programs:**
   Explore rent-to-own or housing grants (see Appendix B). Even modest transitions toward ownership eliminate the constant fear of eviction.

Result: These tactics can reduce your rent burden by 25–60%, freeing hundreds or even thousands of dollars monthly to reinvest in autonomy.

Part 4: The Systems Approach — Combining All Three

Once you begin integrating all three—water, electricity, and rent—you'll notice compounding effects:

- Reduced **utility stress** improves sleep and health.
- Lower bills create emergency savings buffers.
- Smaller living spaces require less energy and maintenance, amplifying every other saving.
- Family unity grows when simplicity replaces financial strain.

You are not just lowering expenses—you're *engineering resilience.*

Part 5: Psychological Rewards of the Bill-Slayer Lifestyle

Cutting bills isn't about stinginess—it's about sovereignty. Each reduction equals:

- More control over your calendar.
- Less fear of job loss.
- Greater ability to pursue creative or family goals.

The act of consciously lowering consumption rewires your brain for freedom. What begins as budgeting becomes a spiritual act of release—you stop leaking energy into systems that no longer serve you.

Journal Prompts: The Bill-Slayer's Reflection

1. Which bill (water, electricity, or rent) feels most "untouchable," and why?
2. How much energy—mental and emotional—do I spend each month worrying about these payments?
3. What quick actions could reduce at least one utility bill within seven days?
4. How does my home layout contribute to waste, and how could I redesign it?
5. What creative or barter-based ways could I reduce rent or exchange value?
6. How would my mindset change if I viewed every bill as a *negotiation*, not a fixed demand?
7. Which appliance or behavior wastes the most resources—and how can I turn that into a challenge to fix?
8. What long-term systems (solar, rainwater collection, energy efficiency) could I begin planning today?
9. How would it feel to live in a home where every bill was cut by half—what would I do with that freedom?
10. How can I celebrate savings not with spending, but with peace, gratitude, and presence?

Closing Reflection

Mastering your bills is not just about saving money—it's about reclaiming life. Every gallon of water saved, every watt reduced, every rent dollar negotiated is a piece of your freedom returned.

You are not here to be a permanent tenant of systems designed to drain you. You are here to become **so efficient, so aware, and so self-sustaining** that even your bills bow to your design.

Chapter 6: Community Leverage — Building Collective Resilience Beyond the Bill

You can only optimize your personal systems so far. True financial freedom begins when you stop trying to do everything *alone.* The greatest untapped source of wealth in modern life isn't hidden in the stock market—it's hidden in **community**.

We live in a world where isolation is marketed as independence. The "self-made" myth glorifies solitary success while the system quietly ensures no one can survive without it. But historically, human societies thrived not through competition—but through *connection.* Shared tools, bartered skills, and local support networks kept people fed, housed, and safe long before the first paycheck ever existed.

This chapter shows how to **rebuild that lost infrastructure of mutual wealth**—how to use networks, neighbors, and local systems to multiply your savings, share resources, and create true resilience that no economic crash or corporate layoff can destroy.

The Philosophy of Communal Autonomy

Individual savings are fragile; collective savings are indestructible. When you share skills, swap goods, and exchange energy locally, you're no longer playing the same financial game. You are building an **alternative economy**—one where trust replaces transactions, and relationships become assets.

Community leverage is about transforming your neighborhood, family, or friend group from a loose collection of individuals into an **interconnected ecosystem** of shared abundance.

Think of it this way: one person can patch a leak; ten people can build a water system. One person can save $50; ten can save thousands through coordinated effort.

Part I: The Power of Networks

1. Skill Exchange Circles

Everyone has a skill—mechanical, digital, domestic, artistic, or logistical. In a community economy, these skills become currency.

How It Works:

- Create a local or online network (group chat, Facebook group, bulletin board).
- Members list skills or services they can offer—childcare, repairs, tutoring, gardening, etc.
- Exchanges are made through barter, rotation, or small cash contributions.

Why It Works:

When ten people each contribute two hours of skill a month, that's 240 collective labor hours exchanged per year—without spending a single extra dollar.

Example:

Maria designs logos for free in exchange for handyman work on her porch. Her neighbor teaches guitar to Maria's son. Value circulates endlessly.

2. Neighborhood Tool Libraries

The average household owns $1,000–$3,000 worth of tools, most of which sit unused 90% of the time. Multiply that across one block, and you've got a warehouse's worth of idle resources.

Start a Tool Library:

- Pool unused tools with neighbors.
- Label and track them using a simple spreadsheet or app.
- Schedule "maintenance weekends" where everyone repairs or sharpens communal items.

Result:

No one buys duplicates, repairs become shared events, and community trust grows.

3. Cooperative Buying Power

You can save enormous amounts by buying in bulk—but most individuals don't have storage or upfront cash to do it alone. That's where **buying co-ops** come in.

Examples:

- Split wholesale grocery orders between 5–10 families.
- Share subscription services (business software, family plans).
- Purchase bulk firewood, heating oil, or garden supplies collectively.

Impact:

Communities often save **20–40% per product**—while reducing packaging waste and delivery costs.

Part II: The Local System Advantage

1. Community Gardens and Food Networks

Food insecurity and grocery inflation can devastate household budgets. Community agriculture is the antidote.

Build or Join a Community Garden:

- Find unused land (churches, schools, city lots).
- Pool seeds, tools, and labor.
- Share harvests or sell extras at a local market.

Expansion Ideas:

- Food swap events for excess produce or canned goods.
- "Harvest shares" where each participant receives a box of community-grown food weekly.
- Compost cooperatives to recycle organic waste into soil wealth.

Result:

Families save hundreds yearly, eat healthier, and form friendships rooted in self-sufficiency.

2. Energy Collectives and Shared Solar

Electric companies profit from isolation. But when neighbors combine resources, power costs can plummet.

Options Include:

- **Shared Solar Programs:** Install a single solar array across multiple properties and divide output or savings.
- **Community Energy Co-Ops:** Pool funds to invest in renewable projects and receive dividends or reduced rates.
- **Neighborhood Efficiency Drives:** Bulk purchase weatherproofing, insulation, or efficient appliances at reduced rates.

Case Example:

In Vermont, a 12-home neighborhood invested collectively in a small solar farm. Each resident now saves 30% on power and receives annual dividends from energy credit sales.

3. Housing Cooperatives and Shared Living Models

Rent doesn't have to be an individual burden. Housing co-ops are structured around shared ownership, lower costs, and democratic decision-making.

Models Include:

- **Co-Living Homes:** Private rooms, shared kitchens, utilities split evenly.
- **Resident-Owned Communities:** Tenants collectively buy the building or land from the landlord, fixing costs long-term.
- **Extended Family Housing:** Three-generation homes that share childcare, cooking, and expenses.

Outcome:

Rent, utilities, and maintenance drop dramatically—while emotional and social resilience rises.

Part III: Mutual Aid and Shared Safety Nets

A true resilient community doesn't wait for crises—it *builds buffers together.*

1. Emergency Funds & Community Trust Banks

- Small neighborhood fund (each member contributes $10–20 monthly).
- Used for medical bills, food shortages, or unexpected crises.
- Governed transparently with group consent.

This micro-system can replace payday loans or high-interest credit cards during emergencies.

2. Shared Childcare Networks

Childcare is one of the largest expenses in modern families. A cooperative childcare exchange allows parents to rotate supervision responsibilities safely.

Model:

Five families each take one weekday for group childcare—saving everyone four days' worth of fees weekly.

3. Health and Resource Sharing

Pooling unused medical supplies, wellness equipment, or supplements helps lower individual costs. Some communities even host **free swap days** for over-the-counter goods or first-aid kits.

Part IV: Digital Neighborhoods and the Rise of Networked Independence

If your local area isn't cohesive yet, the internet can simulate a new kind of "digital village."

Start Online Networks for:

- Bartering services (use platforms like Buy Nothing or local subreddits).
- Finding used/free furniture and home goods.
- Creating group challenges: "No-Spend Month," "Energy-Saving February," "Community Budget Challenge."

The Goal:

Turn digital interaction into physical empowerment—don't just scroll, *swap.*

Part V: From Isolation to Interdependence

Interdependence doesn't mean weakness—it's strategic strength. Every thriving civilization, from small tribes to massive cities, was built on shared systems of trust and cooperation.

When you participate in community leverage:

- Your costs drop.
- Your stress decreases.
- Your access to skills, goods, and opportunities multiplies.
- You stop depending solely on corporations or fragile economies.

You move from consumer to *citizen of a micro-economy.*

Part VI: Building the New Local Economy

Once communities reach critical participation, new possibilities appear:

- **Community Markets:** Cash-light exchanges of produce, crafts, and services.
- **Local Currencies or Credit Systems:** Internal vouchers or time-banking that circulate within the network.
- **Skill Schools:** Teaching trades, financial literacy, gardening, or repair classes—keeping wisdom circulating locally.
- **Repair Cafés:** Monthly meetups where volunteers fix electronics, furniture, and clothing for free.

Each initiative weakens the grip of dependency and replaces it with **localized prosperity.**

Journal Prompts: Building Your Community Leverage

1. Who in my neighborhood or network has practical skills I could learn from or trade with?
2. What resources or items do I own that sit unused but could serve others?
3. What local groups, libraries, or online communities could form the nucleus of a cooperative network?
4. How could I initiate a neighborhood resource share without seeming intrusive?
5. What fears or pride stop me from asking for help or collaboration?
6. How might our collective bills, food, or childcare costs drop if we worked together?
7. What could a "community emergency fund" look like on my block or online group?
8. How could we create shared joy—events, potlucks, challenges—that build financial *and emotional* wealth?
9. What would a "moneyless week" look like with full community support?
10. How can I turn my neighborhood from a group of strangers into a living, breathing safety net?

Final Reflection: From Survival to Solidarity

Freedom is not isolation—it's **connection without control**. When people unite under shared values of simplicity, trust, and mutual aid, they build wealth that money can't measure.

In the age of automation and corporate monopolies, communities that collaborate will not just survive—they will thrive. They will grow their own food, share their tools, cut their bills, and protect each other from the tides of economic instability.

The future of financial freedom is not individual—it's **interdependent**. And when you stop competing with your neighbors and start *creating with them,* you don't just save money—you rebuild society from the ground up.

Chapter 7: New Ways to Earn Without Employers

The system taught us that "a job" is the only safe path. School prepared us to be employable, not independent. The 9-to-5 model conditioned us to think someone else must grant us permission to earn, to be useful, or to have value. But that model is collapsing.

The modern economy no longer rewards obedience—it rewards *creativity, adaptability, and ownership.* The good news? You don't need to wait for an employer to validate your worth. You can build income streams that flow directly to you—without punching a clock, attending pointless meetings, or begging for raises that never match inflation.

This chapter is your detailed roadmap to creating **autonomous income systems**—ways to earn ethically, creatively, and sustainably outside traditional employment.

Part I: The Shift from Job Mindset to Ownership Mindset

Before you can create income, you must redefine what "work" even means.

Traditional employment teaches *dependency*:

- You sell time for a fixed wage.
- Your energy is controlled by someone else's schedule.
- You build wealth for others, not yourself.

Independent earning teaches *agency*:

- You trade value for income.
- You control when, how, and with whom you work.
- You build wealth systems that grow without your constant presence.

The transition starts mentally. You must stop thinking like an employee and start thinking like a **value architect**. Ask not, "Who will hire me?" but "Who can benefit from what I create?"

Part II: Income Without Employers — The Five Freedom Pillars

These are the five core categories of earning independently. You can build one or combine several for resilience and diversity.

1. Skill Monetization: Turning What You Know Into Income

You already have knowledge someone will pay for. The key is packaging it.

Examples:

- **Freelancing:** Offer writing, design, editing, translation, coding, or admin services on platforms like Fiverr, Upwork, or through direct outreach.
- **Micro-Consulting:** Teach small business owners what you already know—marketing, organization, budgeting, time management.
- **Digital Tutoring or Coaching:** Tutor students or teach adults online through marketplaces or your own site.

Strategy:

- Start with one clear service.
- Offer value-driven packages ("3 social media posts for $50") instead of hourly labor.
- Collect testimonials and grow through referrals.

Why it Works:
The global economy increasingly values *skills*, not *degrees.* One strong skill can replace a full-time job if leveraged wisely.

2. The Digital Creator Economy

If you have ideas, insights, or creativity, you can monetize attention. The creator economy rewards individuals who teach, entertain, or inspire.

Paths Include:

- **YouTube & Podcasts:** Build an audience around your expertise, story, or passion. Ad revenue, sponsorships, or memberships can scale.
- **Ebooks & Courses:** Package what you know into teachable products on Gumroad, Teachable, or Etsy.
- **Blogging & Affiliate Marketing:** Review products, write guides, or share advice and earn commission on sales.
- **Newsletter Independence:** A loyal 1,000 subscribers paying $5/month = $5,000/month in passive income.

Pro Tip: Consistency beats perfection. Focus on *serving a niche audience well*, not pleasing everyone.

3. The Ownership Economy — Assets that Earn for You

Instead of selling time, build or buy things that generate money while you sleep.

Examples:

- **Digital Products:** Templates, ebooks, printables, or designs sold repeatedly online.
- **Rental Assets:** Rent out a spare room, vehicle, or tools.
- **Royalties:** Earn from art, books, music, or licensing.
- **Small Investments:** Dividend stocks, REITs, or peer-to-peer lending (start small; scale slow).

Mindset Shift:

Employers pay for your *time* once. Assets pay you *forever*. Build what works while you sleep.

4. Local Microbusiness Models

Not all freedom is digital. Some of the most stable independent earners thrive through **localized micro-enterprises**—small, flexible, high-value ventures rooted in community.

Examples:

- **Mobile Services:** Cleaning, handyman work, laundry, dog walking, delivery, tutoring, or car detailing.
- **Pop-Up Businesses:** Farmers' market booths, food stands, thrift resales, or crafts.
- **Subscription Neighborhood Services:** Offer recurring help (e.g., "Weekly Lawn & Garden Care," "Monthly Declutter Help").
- **Repair & Reuse:** In a world of disposability, fixing things is a rare, profitable skill.

Freedom Principle: A microbusiness with 10 loyal local clients can replace a paycheck while keeping your schedule yours.

5. The Peer-to-Peer (P2P) and Cooperative Economy

The "new economy" is no longer controlled by corporations—it's powered by connection. Use digital platforms and shared systems to build **income through collaboration** instead of subordination.

Examples:

- **Reselling & Reuse:** Flip items on eBay, Mercari, or Facebook Marketplace. Turn thrift into profit.
- **Peer Rentals:** Lend tools, parking spaces, or equipment through apps or locally.
- **Skill-Sharing Circles:** Trade or teach services and charge small community fees.
- **Cooperative Projects:** Join or start local co-ops—shared farms, maker spaces, or artist collectives that share profit.

Why it Works:

P2P systems cut out middlemen. You and your peers directly exchange value without corporate interference.

Part III: Reframing Risk — The Safety of Self-Sufficiency

Most people fear leaving employers because they believe jobs equal safety. Yet modern employment is *not* secure—it's just familiar. You can be replaced, outsourced, or laid off at any moment.

Creating independent income streams distributes your risk. When you rely on multiple systems—your own projects, freelance work, small assets—you're no longer one decision away from zero income. You're **antifragile**: disruption becomes opportunity.

Your new rule: Never depend on one stream. Aim for *three or more modest ones* that together exceed your living costs.

Part IV: Building Your Personal Economy Step-by-Step

Here's a practical roadmap to begin earning independently within 90 days.

Step 1: Identify Your Leverage Skills

List everything you can do that saves someone time, makes them money, or entertains them. Don't undervalue soft skills—organization, storytelling, or empathy can be monetized through coaching, writing, or teaching.

Step 2: Simplify and Focus

Pick *one* income path to start. Too many ideas kill execution. Choose the one that feels most natural to you and easiest to test.

Step 3: Prototype Your First Offer

Create something small and testable:

- A $10 ebook.
- A $25 local service.
- A single consultation.
- A one-week YouTube video challenge.

Success or failure doesn't matter—data does.

Step 4: Reinvest, Don't Inflate

Use early profits to build systems—automation, better tools, or marketing. Resist the urge to upgrade lifestyle. That's how financial independence compounds.

Step 5: Expand into Systems

Once one stream stabilizes, build the next.

For example:

- Start freelancing.
- Package your process into an ebook or course.
- Use the profits to fund digital or physical assets.
  This stacking model creates a *web of wealth* that sustains you indefinitely.

Part V: The Psychological Barriers to Freedom
Breaking away from employers isn't just logistical—it's emotional.

Common Fears:

- "What if I fail?" — You already survive failure daily at work; you just call it 'meetings.'
- "I'm not good enough." — You don't need to be perfect; you need to be *useful.*
- "It's too risky." — Relying on one paycheck is riskier than multiple small streams.
- "I don't have time." — You do. Reclaim your commute, TV time, or social scrolling.

Independent earning isn't harder—it's simply *truer.* It demands courage, consistency, and creativity, not credentials.

Part VI: Ethical Earning in the New Economy

When you work outside traditional structures, you also gain the chance to align income with integrity. You choose:

- Who you serve.
- What values you represent.
- Whether your business heals or harms.

Freedom doesn't just mean working for yourself—it means **working for something that matters.**

- Support sustainability.
- Build human connection instead of exploitation.
- Teach others what you've learned once you succeed.

This is how new economies are born—from individuals who refuse to sell their souls for salaries.

Part VII: Case Studies in Workless Wealth

Case 1 – The Freelancer Farmer:
Jamie left his marketing job to freelance remotely while maintaining a half-acre garden. Between digital clients and local produce sales, his income surpassed his old salary—but his stress disappeared.

Case 2 – The Family Micro-Enterprise:
A single mother and her two teens started a home-based candle and soap shop. They used thrifted materials and social media. Within a year, they paid off debt and reduced their work hours by half.

Case 3 – The Digital Elder:
Retired teacher Rosa began writing and selling short guides on self-sufficiency. Her ebooks sell modestly but consistently—funding her retirement while sharing her wisdom globally.

Lesson:
Freedom is not fantasy. It's a formula—*value, creativity, and persistence.*

Journal Prompts: Designing Your Independent Income

1. What am I skilled at that others constantly ask me for help with?
2. What problems or frustrations do I see every day that I could help solve?
3. How could I turn my current job tasks into freelance or self-run services?
4. What digital or physical assets could I create once and sell many times?
5. Who could benefit most from what I already know?
6. What would my ideal "workday" look like if no boss or commute existed?
7. What small income test could I launch within 14 days to prove my potential?
8. How can I diversify income streams to become antifragile?
9. What ethical boundaries must I keep while building independence?
10. What does "enough" income look like for me—and how can I reach it sustainably?

Closing Reflection: You Are the Economy Now

The old world said: "Find a job."
The new world says: "Create value."

The old system needs you to stay dependent so it can survive.
The new system—*your system*—grows stronger the freer you become.

When you learn to earn without employers, you reclaim your time, your dignity, and your destiny. You stop selling your hours and start owning your life.

The future of work isn't about employment—it's about **empowerment.** And your first dollar earned outside the system will feel like a revolution.

Chapter 8: Permanent Freedom Mode — The Architecture of a Self-Sustaining Life

Most people dream of freedom as an event—a single day when the job ends, the bills stop, and life finally begins. But real, *permanent* freedom isn't a vacation. It's a design system. It's a set of daily, repeatable, intelligent behaviors that make dependency impossible.

Permanent Freedom Mode is not a fantasy of endless leisure; it's a *discipline of sovereignty.* It's the state in which your time, income, energy, and identity are completely under your control—not your employer's, not your creditors', not the government's, and not the algorithm's. It's where survival ends and self-direction begins.

This chapter will teach you how to **build, automate, and protect a self-sustaining lifestyle**, so that you never again depend on unstable jobs, rent panic, or toxic systems to live well.

Part I: What Permanent Freedom Really Means

Freedom isn't the absence of work—it's the absence of coercion.

When you live in Permanent Freedom Mode, every choice—how you earn, where you live, what you consume, and how you spend your time—is made consciously. There's no debt dictating your options, no boss defining your worth, no calendar you don't own.

It's the phase of life where **systems replace stress.** You stop reacting to emergencies and start designing your own economy, your own environment, and your own rhythm.

The four pillars of Permanent Freedom Mode are:

1. **Autonomous Income** – Your earnings come from sources you control, not employers.
2. **Self-Regulating Costs** – Your living expenses are intentionally low, stable, and predictable.
3. **Redundant Systems** – You have backups for everything: food, shelter, power, and money.
4. **Psychological Immunity** – You are no longer emotionally manipulated by fear of loss or scarcity.

Freedom isn't built once—it's maintained daily.

Part II: The Economic Core — Income that Defends Itself

To sustain freedom, your income must no longer depend on your constant labor. Every dollar should either protect or produce the next one.

1. The Three-Tier Income Model

Permanent freedom requires three interconnected types of income:

- **Active Income:** Your current, direct effort—freelance, services, or creative work. (Your short-term engine.)
- **Semi-Passive Income:** Systems that generate money with light maintenance—digital products, recurring memberships, small business automation. (Your medium-term shield.)
- **Passive Income:** Investments, royalties, or peer assets that produce money without your daily input. (Your long-term foundation.)

Together, they create a financial ecosystem that functions even if one stream stops.

2. Diversification through Autonomy

Instead of multiple *jobs*, aim for multiple *self-owned systems.* A person with five small autonomous streams is safer than a person with one "stable" employer.

Examples:

- A minimalist YouTube channel teaching budgeting.
- A small Etsy shop selling templates.
- A rental space shared on Airbnb.
- A coaching micro-service by appointment.
- A $2,000 emergency fund earning interest.

Each system is small, but combined, they produce *financial independence without corporate dependence.*

Part III: The Lifestyle Blueprint — Low Overhead, High Freedom

You can't buy freedom—you subtract your way into it. Permanent Freedom Mode depends on radical control of your **burn rate** (the cost of your daily life).

1. Housing as a Choice, Not a Chain

Your home should never own you. In Permanent Freedom Mode:

- Rent or own something small, efficient, and mobile.
- Favor spaces you can afford on your *lowest* earning month, not your highest.
- Design your home for multiple uses—living, creating, working, storing.

A flexible home base gives you financial agility—if income changes, your life doesn't collapse.

2. Minimalism as an Economic Weapon

Every object you remove reduces insurance, maintenance, cleaning, and clutter. Living light is not deprivation—it's insulation from chaos.

3. Food and Utility Independence

- Cook simple, home-based meals; batch-prep weekly.
- Grow what you can (even herbs on windowsills).
- Use solar or efficient power sources where possible.
- Recycle greywater and collect rain where legal.
  Every autonomy system is a quiet act of rebellion against inflation.

Part IV: The Emotional Code — Mastering the Inner Game of Freedom

You can't live free externally if you're enslaved internally. Permanent Freedom Mode requires **emotional discipline** as much as financial.

1. Deprogram the Scarcity Reflex

The old system trained you to equate stillness with failure. You must rewire your nervous system to see calm as success, not danger.

Meditation, solitude, journaling, and slow mornings become **strategic rituals**—they remind your body that life doesn't have to be hurried to be valuable.

2. Detach Identity from Labor

Your value does not fluctuate with your productivity. Freedom means you can rest without guilt, create without pressure, and earn without servitude.

3. Choose Peace Over Performance

In Permanent Freedom Mode, you stop chasing validation. The applause of strangers, the envy of peers, the illusion of "more" become irrelevant. You measure wealth in clarity, not currency.

Part V: The Systemization of Freedom

Permanent Freedom Mode is sustained by systems that think for you. Once created, they operate even while you sleep.

1. Automate Repetition

Anything you do more than twice should be systemized.

- Bills auto-paid.
- Savings auto-deposited.
- Content auto-scheduled.
- Tasks automated through digital tools.

Automation isn't just convenience—it's *mental liberation*.

2. Simplify Decision Fatigue

Freedom thrives in clarity.

- Wear a small wardrobe of favorite clothes.
- Eat similar healthy meals.
- Keep consistent sleep and work patterns.

You're designing *predictability* in small areas so your creative and strategic energy can focus on growth.

3. Create Emergency Independence Protocols
Have contingency plans for:

- Income disruptions.
- Power or water outages.
- Sudden relocations.

When emergencies happen, you respond, not react. That's the difference between "free" and "frantic."

Part VI: Social Freedom — Rebuilding Community on Your Terms

Permanent freedom doesn't mean isolation—it means **sovereign belonging**.

- **Choose Allies, Not Audiences:** Build networks based on trust and mutual value, not status.
- **Engage in Reciprocity:** Exchange time, knowledge, and help freely.
- **Exit Toxic Environments:** Refuse to participate in drama, exploitation, or envy economies.

Your social ecosystem should amplify peace, not drain it.

Part VII: The Legacy of Permanent Freedom

Once your systems are stable, the final phase begins: **use your freedom to create meaning.**

True liberation isn't about escape—it's about *impact without compromise.*

- Mentor others in escaping the cycle.
- Fund local or global causes that align with your values.
- Create art, innovation, or education that outlives you.

Permanent Freedom Mode transforms you from a survivor into a **source.** You become proof that independence is possible, ethical, and repeatable.

Part VIII: The Freedom Maintenance Rituals

Freedom fades without reinforcement. These rituals keep your independence alive:

1. **Weekly Reset:** Review your finances, projects, and energy. Simplify one thing each week.
2. **Monthly Audit:** Track expenses, cancel waste, and adjust goals.
3. **Quarterly Recharge:** Take short "off-grid" weeks—no screens, no schedules.
4. **Annual Reinvention:** Review what no longer fits your life. Freedom evolves; update your systems accordingly.

Freedom isn't static—it's alive, adaptive, and self-renewing.

Journal Prompts: Building and Sustaining Permanent Freedom Mode

1. What does freedom *feel* like in my body—not just look like on paper?
2. Which recurring fears still anchor me to dependency?
3. What would my week look like if I never had to trade time for survival again?
4. Which systems (income, housing, utilities, routines) could I automate or simplify this month?
5. Who drains my energy, and who restores it?
6. What would my life cost if I only kept what truly mattered?
7. How can I ensure that every dollar I spend builds more freedom, not more obligation?
8. What would a "perfectly free" day look like—hour by hour?
9. How can I make my income streams self-sustaining within the next year?
10. How will I use my freedom to uplift others once I have it?

Final Reflection: Freedom as a Practice, Not a Prize

Permanent Freedom Mode is the point where life stops being a race and becomes a rhythm. You no longer run from scarcity—you walk toward sovereignty. You are not surviving the system; you are transcending it.

Each decision, each simplification, and each act of autonomy becomes a stone in the foundation of a life you control completely.

Freedom isn't something you win—it's something you *tend to.*
And when you maintain it daily—with awareness, purpose, and courage—your life ceases to be a reaction to the world.

It becomes its own world.
Your world.
Built. Owned. And lived—entirely on your terms.

Appendix A: The 6-Month Work Exit Blueprint

Escaping the traditional job system is not an impulsive leap—it's a structured transition. The secret to freedom is not quitting tomorrow; it's **engineering your exit so well that your income, stability, and sanity remain intact.**

This six-month blueprint walks you through the exact psychological, financial, and logistical stages required to move from employee to independent earner. Each month builds on the previous one, layering preparation, skill, and systems until your dependence on employers is gone for good.

The goal is not just to quit a job. It's to **replace the job with an ecosystem**—a sustainable lifestyle and income system that you own completely.

Phase 1 — Month 1: Awareness and Audit

Objective: Understand your true financial, emotional, and skill position. You cannot escape what you haven't measured.

1. The Financial Reality Check

- Print or download the past 3 months of bank and credit statements.
- Categorize all expenses: survival (food, housing, utilities), comfort (subscriptions, entertainment), and excess (status purchases).
- Identify your "true living cost"—the amount you *must* cover each month to live safely.
- Calculate your **Freedom Number:** multiply that figure by 1.5. That's the income goal that gives you security and breathing room after quitting.

2. Skill Inventory

- Write down every task you perform at work, every hobby, and every life skill.
- Next to each, ask: *Could someone pay for this directly?* If yes, it's monetizable.
- Rank them by confidence and enjoyment. The top three become your **initial income pillars.**

3. Psychological Preparation

- Begin "mental detachment." Spend 10 minutes daily visualizing life outside your job—where you live, how you earn, what peace feels like.
- Recognize the difference between fear of change and genuine risk. Fear is emotional noise; risk can be managed.

End-of-Month Goal: A clear picture of your finances, skillset, and mental readiness.

Phase 2 — Month 2: Simplify and Shrink the Burn Rate

Objective: Lower your expenses by 30–50% so you can survive comfortably on less income during transition.

1. Minimalist Overhaul

- Cancel or pause every non-essential subscription and recurring payment.
- Switch to prepaid cell plans, basic streaming tiers, and shared services.
- Audit groceries—plan weekly meals around staples (rice, beans, grains, frozen vegetables).

2. Housing and Transportation

- Explore downsizing, subleasing, or moving closer to low-cost areas.
- Sell unused items or tools; convert clutter into early savings.
- Consider selling a second car or switching to shared transport.

3. Emergency Cushion

- Save at least one month of living expenses. This is not optional—it's the buffer between courage and panic.

4. Energy Management

- Begin setting boundaries at work. Reduce overtime, decline unnecessary commitments, and reclaim mental bandwidth for your exit plan.

End-of-Month Goal: 25–50% lower living costs and the first layer of a safety buffer.

Phase 3 — Month 3: Build Your Micro-Income Foundation
Objective: Create your first *independent dollar.*

1. Choose Your Primary Income Vehicle
From your skill audit, pick one monetizable path:

- Freelancing or consulting
- Online teaching or digital products
- Local services or resale
- Micro-business or craft production

2. Launch a Prototype Offer

- Create one service or product you can sell within two weeks.
- Price it simply: low enough to attract clients, high enough to feel real.
- Test it through personal networks, local listings, or online marketplaces.

3. Reinforce Routine

- Dedicate one hour before or after work daily to your project.
- Use weekends for content, outreach, and improvement.
- Log every sale or client inquiry—momentum is your proof of possibility.

4. Document Systems
Keep track of repeatable steps. This documentation will form the foundation for automation later.

End-of-Month Goal: First independent sales or client work; proof that income can be generated without your employer.

Phase 4 — Month 4: Strengthen and Scale
Objective: Transform early wins into reliable systems.

1. Refine Your Offer

- Gather feedback from your first customers or clients.
- Adjust pricing and delivery based on effort vs. reward.
- Identify what sells easiest and requires the least effort.

2. Build Support Infrastructure

- Create basic branding (website, portfolio, or social page).
- Set up a dedicated bank account and bookkeeping tool.
- Automate tasks like invoices, emails, and social scheduling.

3. Multiply Streams

- Add a complementary income source that aligns with your first (e.g., if you freelance, create a related digital product).
- Diversify enough that one loss won't halt progress.

4. Reinforce Savings
Deposit 30–40% of all new earnings into your freedom fund. Your goal by month's end is **three months of essential expenses saved.**

End-of-Month Goal: Stable side income covering at least 25–40% of your monthly costs.

Phase 5 — Month 5: Transition Logistics and Psychological Exit

Objective: Prepare your life, network, and mind for departure.

1. Calculate the Crossover Point

When your independent income plus savings can cover 75–100% of monthly essentials for 3–6 months, you've reached the **Crossover Point.**

2. Build an Exit Timeline

- Decide on your resignation date (preferably at the end of a pay period).
- Draft a professional, minimal notice letter.
- Secure essential contacts, testimonials, or references while relations are good.

3. Strengthen Your Ecosystem

- Inform trusted allies of your plans—avoid gossip, but build support.
- Join online or local self-employed communities for accountability.
- Establish weekly work rhythms that mirror your upcoming solo life.

4. Emotional Detachment Ritual

Create a symbolic "release" ritual before resigning—journaling, shredding old work notes, a solo day trip, or a gratitude list. Leave mentally before you leave physically.

End-of-Month Goal: Your exit date is fixed, your financial safety net solid, and your confidence rooted in evidence—not hope.

Phase 6 — Month 6: Execute the Exit and Build Permanent Freedom Mode

Objective: Leave employment gracefully, stabilize independence, and lock in new systems of control.

1. The Final Notice

- Give two to four weeks' notice with professionalism.
- Avoid emotional outbursts or detailed explanations; your dignity is part of your brand.
- Secure all owed payments, benefits, or unused leave.

2. Post-Exit Stabilization

- Transition immediately into your established daily structure: morning planning, focused creation, afternoon outreach, evening accounting.
- Reinvest profits into business tools, savings, and debt elimination.
- Keep expenses frozen at your Month-2 levels until income triples.

3. System Automation

- Automate client onboarding, payment processing, or product delivery.
- Schedule marketing content 30 days in advance.
- Use recurring billing or subscription systems where possible.

4. Redefine Success

- Success is no longer a paycheck. It's waking up with ownership of your hours.
- Maintain your self-employment journal: record lessons, ideas, and gratitude daily.
- Review your six-month transformation and set one-year vision goals.

End-of-Month Goal: You have fully exited the job system, stabilized independent income, and begun your life in **Permanent Freedom Mode.**

Freedom Maintenance Principles (Post-Exit)

To prevent regression into dependence, practice these ongoing disciplines:

1. **Keep Costs Grounded.** Lifestyle inflation is the fastest path back to slavery.
2. **Save Before You Scale.** Double your savings before doubling your spending.
3. **Diversify Streams.** Three to five income flows ensure long-term resilience.
4. **Protect Your Energy.** Work for yourself, not against your health.
5. **Automate Everything Repetitive.** Automation keeps your freedom scalable.
6. **Give Back.** Teach others the path you walked; generosity multiplies stability.

Six-Month Exit Checklist Summary

◈ Month 1: Full financial and skill audit completed.
◈ Month 2: 25–50% cost reduction and one-month emergency fund built.
◈ Month 3: First independent sales or freelance income earned.
◈ Month 4: Side income covering 25–40% of expenses; savings at three months.
◈ Month 5: Exit date scheduled; ecosystem and routines solidified.
◈ Month 6: Formal resignation executed; independent systems fully operational.

Final Word: From Employee to Architect

Leaving the work system is not rebellion—it's redesign.
You are not quitting work; you are **reclaiming authorship** over it.

In six focused months, you can transition from surviving on wages to thriving on wisdom, from clocking in to creating out, and from fear of the unknown to mastery of your own economy.

Your six-month exit is not the end of work—it's the beginning of **work that serves you.**
Permanent Freedom Mode begins here.

Appendix B: 101 Income-Generating Micro Projects

You don't need venture capital, degrees, or full-time staff to make money—you need **micro momentum.**

Micro projects are small, low-risk, quick-to-launch income experiments that teach you how to earn **without employers.** They cost little, scale fast, and build confidence through proof of concept.

Each project below is designed for accessibility: most require less than $200 to start, a few hours of setup, and skills many people already have. They are organized into categories so you can mix digital, creative, physical, and service-based streams.

Section I: Digital Products & Knowledge Assets

1. **E-Book Creation:** Write short guides (3–10k words) on topics you know; sell on Gumroad, Etsy, or Kindle.
2. **Printable Planners:** Design daily, fitness, or budget trackers using Canva; sell as instant downloads.
3. **Micro Courses:** Record 3–5 short lessons teaching a single skill; host on Teachable or Udemy.
4. **Template Packs:** Resume, invoice, or presentation templates for freelancers and small businesses.
5. **Niche Blogs:** Start a blog in a focused niche; monetize with ads or affiliate links.
6. **Email Mini-Course:** Offer a free 5-day tutorial that upsells a paid version.
7. **Digital Journals:** Guided self-discovery or gratitude journals formatted for tablets.
8. **Stock Photography:** Sell thematic photo packs on Adobe Stock or Shutterstock.
9. **Digital Art Prints:** Create wall art, affirmations, or quotes for download.
10. **Spreadsheet Tools:** Budget or calculator sheets built in Google Sheets; sell licenses.
11. **Audio Background Loops:** Create ambient music for creators or gamers.
12. **Podcast Companion PDF:** Turn your podcast episodes into monetized workbooks.
13. **Language Flashcards:** Digital vocabulary decks for learners on Quizlet or Etsy.
14. **Font Creation:** Design a custom font or lettering style for commercial use.
15. **AI Prompt Libraries:** Curate ready-to-use AI prompts for designers, marketers, or writers.

Section II: Freelance & Skill-Based Services

1. **Copyediting / Proofreading:** Offer on Fiverr or directly to indie authors.
2. **Virtual Assistant:** Provide inbox, scheduling, or data entry support remotely.
3. **Social Media Caption Writer:** Manage captions and hashtags for local shops.
4. **Website Setup Assistant:** Use platforms like Wix or Squarespace for non-tech clients.
5. **Resume & LinkedIn Optimization:** Help job seekers rewrite profiles.
6. **Short-Form Video Editor:** Edit Reels, TikToks, or YouTube Shorts for creators.
7. **Podcast Editor:** Clean and format podcast audio files.
8. **Transcription Service:** Convert audio into clean text documents.
9. **Presentation Design:** Beautify PowerPoint decks for professionals.
10. **Email Newsletter Writer:** Curate and send content for small businesses.
11. **Blog Ghostwriter:** Write SEO articles for entrepreneurs.
12. **E-Commerce Product Descriptions:** Rewrite listings for Etsy or Shopify sellers.
13. **Translation or Localization:** Offer bilingual services for global markets.
14. **Online Tutoring:** Teach math, language, or writing via Zoom.
15. **Digital Marketing Assistant:** Run basic Facebook or Google ads for local clients.

Section III: Handmade & Craft-Based Projects

1. **Soy Candles:** Small batches with custom scents and eco packaging.
2. **Handmade Soap Bars:** Use natural oils; sell at markets or online.
3. **Jewelry Micro-Collections:** Create themed sets using inexpensive beads or clay.
4. **Mini Resin Art:** Coasters, keychains, or ornaments.
5. **Customized Mugs or Shirts:** Use print-on-demand platforms like Printful.
6. **Bookmarks & Stationery:** Niche-themed designs (book quotes, fandom art).
7. **Pressed-Flower Frames:** Combine nature and minimalist decor.
8. **Hand-Painted Planters:** Sell locally with small succulents.
9. **Embroidery Patches:** Create unique patches or iron-on art.
10. **Crochet Accessories:** Small wearable items—beanies, mittens, or bags.
11. **Wood-Burned Signs:** Simple home quotes crafted on scrap wood.
12. **Mini Sculpture Figures:** Polymer clay fantasy creatures or mascots.
13. **Calligraphy Services:** Custom envelopes or invitations.
14. **Upcycled Furniture:** Restore or repaint small thrifted pieces for resale.
15. **Fabric Scrap Quilts:** Eco-friendly blankets made from reused materials.

Section IV: Food & Beverage Micro Ventures

1. **Home-Baked Bread:** Sell locally under cottage-food regulations.
2. **Flavored Popcorn Bags:** Unique seasonings for fairs or deliveries.
3. **Homemade Granola or Trail Mix:** Package attractively in jars.
4. **Jam & Preserves:** Local fruit converted into artisanal spreads.
5. **Small-Batch Coffee Blends:** Partner with local roaster for custom branding.
6. **Infused Oils or Vinegars:** Garlic, rosemary, or chili versions for gifts.
7. **Healthy Snack Boxes:** Curated monthly packages for offices.
8. **Custom Spice Blends:** Ethnic or themed seasoning lines.
9. **DIY Hot Chocolate Kits:** Seasonal gifting idea.
10. **Farmers-Market Smoothie Stand:** Blend local produce at pop-ups.

Section V: Local & Physical Services

1. **Pet-Sitting or Dog-Walking:** Build repeat clients through trust.
2. **House-Sitting:** Offer travel coverage for neighbors.
3. **Errand Runner:** Grocery or pharmacy pickup for busy or elderly locals.
4. **Cleaning Microservice:** "$50 two-room refresh" niche.
5. **Laundry & Folding Pickup:** Wash and return within 24 hours.
6. **Yard Cleanup Crew:** Offer spring/fall flat-rate cleanups.
7. **Snow Removal:** Side income in cold seasons with shovel or blower.
8. **Car Detailing:** Mobile washing using minimal supplies.
9. **Furniture Assembly:** Serve people ordering flat-pack furniture.
10. **Gutter Cleaning or Pressure Washing:** Once-a-year jobs with high ROI.
11. **Home Plant Care Service:** Water and tend indoor plants for travelers.
12. **Mobile Notary (where licensed):** Convenient legal signature services.
13. **Event Setup Assistant:** Chairs, tables, decor prep for small gatherings.
14. **Moving Helper:** Packing or loading assistance for local relocations.
15. **Personal Tech Tutor:** Help seniors or small-biz owners use devices.

Section VI: Reselling & Flipping

1. **Thrift-Store Flips:** Buy undervalued clothing or antiques and resell online.
2. **Book Resale:** Used books sourced from libraries or yard sales.
3. **Electronics Refurbish:** Clean, test, and resell older devices.
4. **Free-to-Profit Challenge:** Collect free items from listings; fix and flip.
5. **Vintage Clothing Booth:** Curate 1990s or Y2K trends for resale.
6. **Sneaker Cleaning & Resale:** Restore scuffed pairs for collectors.
7. **Vinyl Record Sales:** Source old records from estate sales.
8. **Collectible Trading Cards:** Buy, grade, and resell niche cards.
9. **Furniture Restoration:** Paint or reupholster small chairs/tables.
10. **Seasonal Decor Flips:** Buy off-season, sell during holidays.

Section VII: Passive & Semi-Passive Micro Systems

1. **Affiliate Blog:** Earn commissions by reviewing tools you use.
2. **Ad Revenue YouTube Shorts:** Daily uploads in evergreen niches.
3. **Niche Newsletter:** Charge small subscriptions for specialized insight.
4. **Print-on-Demand Store:** Merch tied to a hobby or slogan.
5. **Digital Stock Video:** Loop footage for editors and creators.
6. **Domain Flipping:** Buy memorable URLs, resell at premium.
7. **Vending Machine Placement:** One or two machines in high-traffic spots.
8. **ATM Ownership:** Partner with local venues to host your ATM.
9. **Storage Space Rental:** Rent out a garage or shed.
10. **Photography Subscription:** Sell monthly digital calendars or wallpapers.

Section VIII: Creative & Educational Ventures

1. **Children's Story Author:** Self-publish illustrated e-stories.
2. **Music Lessons:** Offer guitar, piano, or vocal coaching at home.
3. **Art Workshops:** Host small painting or craft sessions.
4. **Local History Tours:** Monetize deep knowledge of your city.
5. **Guided Meditation Recordings:** Sell on InsightTimer or your site.
6. **Creative Writing Prompts Journal:** Printable or bound product.
7. **Photography Mini-Sessions:** 15-minute portrait events.
8. **DIY Repair Classes:** Teach sewing, mending, or basic maintenance.
9. **Career Skill Coaching:** Help others learn resume or interview strategy.
10. **Language Conversation Circles:** Paid practice groups online or in cafés.
11. **Community Pop-Up Booth:** A rotating market stall featuring multiple small creators—earn commissions as organizer.

How to Use This List

1. **Choose Three:** Highlight the ideas that excite you *and* match your existing abilities.
2. **Prototype One:** Within seven days, build a minimal version—sell one product or book one client.
3. **Refine Weekly:** Track what works, cut what doesn't, and reinvest small profits.
4. **Stack Streams:** After 3–6 months, maintain 2–3 micro projects to stabilize income.
5. **Automate & Scale:** Systematize the top performer and free your time for new experiments.

Mindset Principles for Micro-Project Success

- **Speed Beats Perfection:** Launch ugly. Learn fast.
- **Solve Real Problems:** Every profitable idea removes friction from someone's life.
- **Keep Costs Tiny:** Use free tools and organic marketing first.
- **Measure in Proof, Not Dreams:** One sale is evidence. Ten sales is validation.
- **Reinvest, Don't Inflate:** Profits fuel freedom, not lifestyle expansion.
- **Teach While You Earn:** Sharing your process attracts clients and collaborators.

Final Note: Your Micro Projects Are the Building Blocks of Freedom

Each micro project is a miniature rebellion against dependence—a proof that your creativity, not your employer, is the real source of wealth.

Start one this week. Even a single $50 project can change your psychology from "I need a paycheck" to **"I can create value."**
Stack ten of them, and you're no longer surviving—you're sovereign.

That's how freedom begins: **one small project at a time, repeated until independence becomes your default mode.**

Message from the Author:

I hope you enjoyed this book, I love astrology and knew there was not a book such as this out on the shelf. I love metaphysical items as well. Please check out my other books:

-Life of Government Benefits

-My life of Hell

-My life with Hydrocephalus

-Red Sky

-World Domination:Woman's rule

-World Domination:Woman's Rule 2: The War

-Life and Banishment of Apophis: book 1

-The Kidney Friendly Diet

-The Ultimate Hemp Cookbook

-Creating a Dispensary(legally)

-Cleanliness throughout life: the importance of showering from childhood to adulthood.

-Strong Roots: The Risks of Overcoddling children

-Hemp Horoscopes: Cosmic Insights and Earthly Healing

- Celestial Hemp Navigating the Zodiac: Through the Green Cosmos

-Astrological Hemp: Aligning The Stars with Earth's Ancient Herb

-The Astrological Guide to Hemp: Stars, Signs, and Sacred Leaves

-Green Growth: Innovative Marketing Strategies for your Hemp Products and Dispensary

-Cosmic Cannabis

-Astrological Munchies

-Henry The Hemp

-Zodiacal Roots: The Astrological Soul Of Hemp

- **Green Constellations: Intersection of Hemp and Zodiac**

-Hemp in The Houses: An astrological Adventure Through The Cannabis Galaxy

-Galactic Ganja Guide

Heavenly Hemp
Zodiac Leaves
Doctor Who Astrology
Cannastrology
Stellar Satvias and Cosmic Indicas
Celestial Cannabis: A Zodiac Journey
AstroHerbology: The Sky and The Soil: Volume 1
AstroHerbology:Celestial Cannabis:Volume 2
Cosmic Cannabis Cultivation
The Starry Guide to Herbal Harmony: Volume 1
The Starry Guide to Herbal Harmony: Cannabis Universe: Volume 2
Yugioh Astrology: Astrological Guide to Deck, Duels and more
Nightmare Mansion: Echoes of The Abyss
Nightmare Mansion 2: Legacy of Shadows
Nightmare Mansion 3: Shadows of the Forgotten
Nightmare Mansion 4: Echoes of the Damned
The Life and Banishment of Apophis: Book 2
Nightmare Mansion: Halls of Despair
Healing with Herb: Cannabis and Hydrocephalus
Planetary Pot: Aligning with Astrological Herbs: Volume 1
Fast Track to Freedom: 30 Days to Financial Independence Using AI, Assets, and Agile Hustles
Cosmic Hemp Pathways
How to Become Financially Free in 30 Days: 10,000 Paths to Prosperity
Zodiacal Herbage: Astrological Insights: Volume 1
Nightmare Mansion: Whispers in the Walls
The Daleks Invade Atlantis
Henry the hemp and Hydrocephalus

10X The Kidney Friendly Diet
Cannabis Universe: Adult coloring book

Hemp Astrology: The Healing Power of the Stars

Zodiacal Herbage: Astrological Insights: Cannabis Universe: Volume 2

Planetary Pot: Aligning with Astrological Herbs: Cannabis Universes: Volume 2

Doctor Who: Convergence Protocol – The Replicator War

Nightmare Mansion: Curse of the Blood Moon

The Celestial Stoner: A Guide to the Zodiac

Cosmic Pleasures: Sex Toy Astrology for Every Sign

Hydrocephalus Astrology: Navigating the Stars and Healing Waters

Lapis and the Mischievous Chocolate Bar

Celestial Positions: Sexual Astrology for Every Sign

Apophis's Shadow Work Journal: **:** A Journey of Self-Discovery and Healing

Kinky Cosmos: Sexual Kink Astrology for Every Sign

Digital Cosmos: The Astrological Digimon Compendium

Stellar Seeds: The Cosmic Guide to Growing with Astrology

Apophis's Daily Gratitude Journal

Cat Astrology: Feline Mysteries of the Cosmos

The Cosmic Kama Sutra: An Astrological Guide to Sexual Positions

Unleash Your Potential: A Guided Journal Powered by AI Insights

Whispers of the Enchanted Grove

Cosmic Pleasures: An Astrological Guide to Sexual Kinks

369, 12 Manifestation Journal

Whisper of the nocturne journal(blank journal for writing or drawing)

The Boogey Book

Locked In Reflection: A Chastity Journey Through Locktober

Generating Wealth Quickly:How to Generate $100,000 in 24 Hours

Star Magic: Harness the Power of the Universe

The Flatulence Chronicles: A Fart Journal for Self-Discovery

The Doctor and The Death Moth

Seize the Day: A Personal Seizure Tracking Journal

The Ultimate Boogeyman Safari: A Journey into the Boogie World and Beyond

Whispers of Samhain: 1,000 Spells of Love, Luck, and Lunar Magic: Samhain Spell Book

Apophis's guides:Witch's Spellbook Crafting Guide for Halloween

Frost & Flame: The Enchanted Yule Grimoire of 1000 Winter Spells

The Ultimate Boogey Goo Guide & Spooky Activities for Halloween Fun

Harmony of the Scales: A Libra's Spellcraft for Balance and Beauty

The Enchanted Advent: 36 Days of Christmas Wonders

Nightmare Mansion: The Labyrinth of Screams

Harvest of Enchantment: 1,000 Spells of Gratitude, Love, and Fortune for Thanksgiving

The Boogey Chronicles: A Journal of Nightly Encounters and Shadowy Secrets

The 12 Days of Financial Freedom: A Step-by-Step Christmas Countdown to Transform Your Finances

Sigil of the Eternal Spiral Blank Journal

A Christmas Feast: Timeless Recipes for Every Meal

Holiday Stress-Free Solutions: A Survival Guide to Thriving During the Festive Season

Yu-Gi-Oh! Holiday Gifting Mastery: The Ultimate Guide for Fans and Newcomers Alike

Holiday Harmony: A Hydrocephalus Survival Guide for the Festive Season

Celestial Craft: The Witch's Almanac for 2025 – A Cosmic Guide to Manifestations, Moons, and Mystical Events

Doctor Who: The Toymaker's Winter Wonderland

Tulsa King Unveiled: A Thrilling Guide to Stallone's Mafia Masterpiece

Pendulum Craft: A Complete Guide to Crafting and Using Personalized Divination Tools

Nightmare Mansion: Santa's Eternal Eve

Starlight Noel: A Cosmic Journey through Christmas Mysteries

The Dark Architect: Unlocking the Blueprint of Existence

Surviving the Embrace: The Ultimate Guide to Encounters with The Hugging Molly

The Enchanted Codex: Secrets of the Craft for Witches, Wiccans, and Pagans

Harvest of Gratitude: A Complete Thanksgiving Guide

Yuletide Essentials: A Complete Guide to an Authentic and Magical Christmas

Celestial Smokes: A Cosmic Guide to Cigars and Astrology

Living in Balance: A Comprehensive Survival Guide to Thriving with Diabetes Insipidus

Cosmic Symbiosis: The Venom Zodiac Chronicles

The Cursed Paw of Ambition

Cosmic Symbiosis: The Astrological Venom Journal

Celestial Wonders Unfold: A Stargazer's Guide to the Cosmos (2024-2029)

The Ultimate Black Friday Prepper's Guide: Mastering Shopping Strategies and Savings

Cosmic Sales: The Astrological Guide to Black Friday Shopping

Legends of the Corn Mother and Other Harvest Myths

Whispers of the Harvest: The Corn Mother's Journal

The Evergreen Spellbook

The Doctor Meets the Boogeyman

The White Witch of Rose Hall's SpellBook

The Gingerbread Golem's Shadow: A Study in Sweet Darkness

The Gingerbread Golem Codex: An Academic Exploration of Sweet Myths

The Gingerbread Golem Grimoire: Sweet Magicks and Spells for the Festive Witch

The Curse of the Gingerbread Golem

10-minute Christmas Crafts for kids

Christmas Crisis Solutions: The Ultimate Last-Minute Survival Guide

Gingerbread Golem Recipes: Holiday Treats with a Magical Twist

The Infinite Key: Unlocking Mystical Secrets of the Ages

Enchanted Yule: A Wiccan and Pagan Guide to a Magical and Memorable Season

Dinosaurs of Power: Unlocking Ancient Magick

Astro-Dinos: The Cosmic Guide to Prehistoric Wisdom

Gallifrey's Yule Logs: A Festive Doctor Who Cookbook

The Dino Grimoire: Secrets of Prehistoric Magick

The Gift They Never Knew They Needed

The Gingerbread Golem's Culinary Alchemy: Enchanting Recipes for a Sweetly Dark Feast

A Time Lord Christmas: Holiday Adventures with the Doctor

Krampusproofing Your Home: Defensive Strategies for Yule

Silent Frights: A Collection of Christmas Creepypastas to Chill Your Bones

Santa Raptor's Jolly Carnage: A Dino-Claus Christmas Tale

Prehistoric Palettes: A Dino Wicca Coloring Journey

The Christmas Wishkeeper Chronicles

The Starlight Sleigh: A Holiday Journey

Elf Secrets: The True Magic of the North Pole

Candy Cane Conjurations

Cooking with Kids: Recipes Under 20 Minutes

Doctor Who: The TARDIS Confiscation

The Anxiety First Aid Kit: Quick Tools to Calm Your Mind

Frosty Whispers: A Winter's Tale

The Infinite Key: Unlocking the Secrets to Prosperity, Resilience, and Purpose

The Grasping Void: Why You'll Regret This Purchase

Astrology for Busy Bees: Star Signs Simplified

The Instant Focus Formula: Cut Through the Noise

The Secret Language of Colors: Unlocking the Emotional Codes

Sacred Fossil Chronicles: Blank Journal

The Christmas Cottage Miracle

Feeding Frenzy: Graboid-Inspired Recipes

Manifest in Minutes: The Quick Law of Attraction Guide

The Symbiote Chronicles: Doctor Who's Venomous Journey

Think Tiny, Grow Big: The Minimalist Mindset

The Energy Key: Unlocking Limitless Motivation

New Year, New Magic: Manifesting Your Best Year Yet

Unstoppable You: Mastering Confidence in Minutes

Infinite Energy: The Secret to Never Feeling Drained

Lightning Focus: Mastering the Art of Productivity in a Distracted World

Saturnalia Manifestation Magick: A Guide to Unlocking Abundance During the Solstice

Graboids and Garland: The Ultimate Tremors-Themed Christmas Guide

12 Nights of Holiday Magic

The Power of Pause: 60-Second Mindfulness Practices

The Quick Reset: How to Reclaim Your Life After Burnout

The Shadow Eater: A Tale of Despair and Survival

The Micro-Mastery Method: Transform Your Skills in Just Minutes a Day

Reclaiming Time: How to Live More by Doing Less

Chronovore: The Eternal Nexus

The Mind Reset: Unlocking Your Inner Peace in a Chaotic World
Confidence Code: Building Unshakable Self-Belief
Baby the Vampire Terrier
Baby the Vampire Terrier's Christmas Adventure
Celestial Streams: The Content Creator's Astrology Manual
The Wealth Whisperer: Unlocking Abundance with Everyday Actions
The Energy Equation: Maximize Your Output Without Burning Out
The Happiness Algorithm: Science-Backed Steps to Joyful Living
Stress-Free Success: Achieving Goals Without Anxiety
Mindful Wealth: The New Blueprint for Financial Freedom
The Festive Flavors of New Year: A Culinary Celebration
The Master's Gambit: Keys of Eternal Power
Shadowed Secrets: Groundhog Day Mysteries
Beneath the Burrow: Lessons from the Groundhog
Spring's Whispers: The Groundhog's Prediction
The Limitless Mindset: Unlock Your Untapped Potential
The Focus Funnel: How to Cut Through Chaos and Get Results
Bold Moves: Building Courage to Live on Your Terms
The Daily Shift: Simple Practices for Lasting Transformation
The Quarter-Life Reset: Thriving in Your 20s and 30s
The Art of Shadowplay: Building Your Own Personal Myth
The Eternal Loop: Finding Purpose in Repetition
Burrowing Wisdom: Life Lessons from the Groundhog
Shadow Work: A Groundhog Day Perspective
Love in Bloom: 5-Minute Romantic Gestures
The Shadowspell Codex: Secrets of Forbidden Magick
The Burnout Cure: Finding Balance in a Busy World
The Groundhog Prophecy: Unlocking Seasonal Secrets
Nog Tales: The Spirited History of Eggnog
Six More Weeks: Embracing Seasonal Transitions
The Lumivian Chronicles: Fragments of the Fifth Dimension

Money on Your Mind: A Beginner's Guide to Wealth
The Focus Fix: Breaking Through Distraction
January's Spirit Keepers: Mystical Protectors of the Cold
Creativity Unchained: Unlocking Your Wildest Ideas in 2025
Manifestation Mastery: 365 Days to Rewrite Your Reality
The Groundhog's Mirror: Reflecting on Change
The Weeping Angels' Christmas Curse
Burrowed in Time: A Groundhog Day Journey
Heartbeats: Poems to Share with Your Valentine
Dino Wicca: The Sacred Grimoire of Prehistoric Magick
Courage of the Pride: Finding Your Inner Roar
The Lion's Leap: Bold Moves for Big Results
Healthy Hustle: Achieving Without Overworking
Practical Manifesting: Turning Dreams into Reality in 2025
Jurassic Pharaohs: Unlocking the Magick of Ancient Egypt and Dino Wicca
The Happiness Equation: Small Changes for Big Joy
The Confidence Compass: Finding Your Inner Strength
Whispers in the Hollow: Tales of the Forgotten Beasts
Echoes from the Hollow: The Return of Forgotten Beasts
The Hollow Ascendant: The Rise of the Forgotten Beasts
The Relationship Reset: Building Better Connections
Mastering the Morning: How to Win the Day Before 8 AM
The Shadow's Dance: Groundhog Day Symbolism
Cupid's Kitchen: Quick Valentine's Day Recipes
Valentine's Day on a Budget: Love Without Breaking the Bank
Astrocraft: Aligning the Stars in the World of Minecraft
Forecasting Life: Groundhog Day Reflections
Bleeding Hearts: Twisted Tales of Valentine's Terror

Herbal Smoke Revolution: The Ultimate Guide to Nature's Cigarette Alternative

Winter's Wrath: The Complete Survival Blueprint for Extreme Freezes.

The Groundhog's Shadow: A Tale of Seasons
Burrowed Insights: Wisdom from the Groundhog
Sensual Strings: The Art of Erotic Bondage
Whispered Flames: Unlocking the Power of Fire Play
Forgotten Shadows: A Guide to Cryptids Lost to Time
Six Weeks of Secrets: Groundhog Day's Hidden Messages
Shadows and Cycles: Groundhog Day Reflections
The Art of Love Letters: Crafting the Perfect Message
Romantic Getaways at Home: Turning Your Space into Paradise
Purrfect Brews: A Cat Lover's Guide to Coffee and Companionship
The Groundhog's Wisdom: Timeless Lessons for Modern Life
The Shadow Oracle: Groundhog Day as a Predictor
Emerging from the Burrow: A Journey of Renewal
The Language of Love: Learning Your Partner's Love Style
Authorpreneur: The Ultimate Blueprint for Writing, Publishing, and Thriving as an Author
Weathering the Seasons: Groundhog Day Perspectives
Valentine's Day Magic: A Guide to Romantic Rituals
The Shadow Chronicles: Stories of Groundhog Day
Love and Laughter: Fun Games for Valentine's Day
AstroRealty: Unlocking the Stars for Property Success
The Groundhog's Path: A Guide to Seasonal Balance
Groundhog Day Diaries: Reflections in the Shadow
The Groundhog's Light: Illuminating the Path Ahead
Valentine's Traditions from Around the World
AI Wealth Revolution: Unlocking the Trillionaire Mindset
Love Rekindled: Reigniting Passion in Relationships
Single and Thriving: Self-Love on Valentine's Day
Emerald Legends: Mystical Tales of Ireland
Green Alchemy: Harnessing Nature's Magic
The Hearts of Horror: A Valentine's Day Nightmare

The Leprechaun's Guide to Wealth and Wisdom

Dancing with the Sidhe: Celebrating the Otherworld

Shamrocks and Shadows: Mysteries of the Green Isle

Emerald Energy: Harnessing Luck and Growth

The Gingerbread Golem's Valentine: A Sweetheart's Guide to Love and Enchantment

The Celtic Knot: Weaving Life and Destiny

Green Fire: Elemental Magic for St. Patrick's Day

Clover Chronicles: Finding Your Inner Luck

Ireland's Mystical Creatures: A Field Guide

Gingerbread Golem's Love Almanac

Prowl and Thrive: The Lion's Guide to Success

Love Alchemy: Transforming Your Life Through Heart Energy

WORLD DOMINATION: Woman's Rule 3:The New Life

The Midnight Rose: A Guide to Lunar Love Spells

The Forbidden Letters: Writing Your Own Love Prophecy

Luck and Lore: St. Patrick's Day for Modern Mystics

The Green Path: A Pagan Celebration of Renewal

The Dark Architect's Guide to Reprogramming Reality

Prankster's Paradise: A Guide to Harmless Hijinks

Manifest Your Reality: The Law of Attraction Simplified

The TARDIS Owner's Manual: Understanding the Doctor's Ship: *A complete guide to the TARDIS, its technology, secrets, and mysteries*

Starlit Romance: Astrology Secrets for Finding True Love

The Time Lord's Atlas: A Complete Guide to the Whoniverse: ***A breakdown of the locations, planets, and dimensions explored in Doctor Who***

Sweetheart Shadows: The Dark Side of Love and Attraction

February Fire: Reigniting Passion in Every Area of Life

The Self-Love Toolkit: 5 Ways to Embrace Who You Are

February Sparks: Ignite Your Dreams in 28 Days

March to Success: A 31-Day Action Blueprint
Ancient Paths: The 13 Sacred Principles of Dino Wicca
Echoes of Tomorrow: Navigating the AI Revolution
The Wellness Blueprint: Balancing Mind, Body, and Soul
Green Horizons: Sustainable Living for a Better Tomorrow
The AI Wealth Code: How to Make Millions with Automation
AI-Powered Creativity: Writing, Art, and Music for Profit
Extinction Rites: Rebirthing Your Soul Through Prehistoric Magick
Sacred Serpents tarot
Celestial Enchantment blank journal
Star Strains
Culinary Journeys: Exploring Global Flavors at Home
The Hollowvale Curse
The Hollowvale Harvest
The Egg of Transformation: Awakening Your Inner Power
Blooming Into Power: A Wiccan Guide to Spring Awakening
The Nightmare Nexus: The Third Doctor's Perilous Haunting
Digital Detox: Reclaiming Your Life in a Connected World
Ostara's Path: Walking the Spiral of Renewal
The Sacred Hare
Financial Freedom: Building Wealth in the Modern Age
Spring's Cauldron: Stirring the Waters of Change
The Hollowvale Pact
Quantum Consciousness: The Science of Reality Shifting
The Hollowvale Hunger
The Sacred Waters Within: A Witch's Guide to Hydrocephalus Magick
The Raven's Nest: Building a Life of Unshakable Stability
AI and the Human Mind: The Future of Intelligence
The Hollowvale Reckoning
Timeless Love: Building and Maintaining Lasting Relationships

The Raven's Roar: Unlocking Unstoppable Confidence

Raven Sight: Awakening Intuition and Inner Wisdom

The Butterfly Effect: Small Changes, Big Transformations

Taming the Boogeyman: How to Conquer Your Inner Fears

The Magick of Green: Awakening Earth's Energy in You

The Entrepreneurial Mindset: Secrets to Business Success

The Hollowvale End

The Shadow Luck Ritual: Reclaiming Power from Your Dark Side

Spring Magick for Beginners: A Simple Guide to Seasonal Energy Work

Doctor Who: The Hollowvale Conundrum

The March of Miracles: Unlocking Synchronicities in Spring

Unveiling the Cosmos: A Guide to Stargazing and Space Exploration

The Ultimate Guide to Surviving an Economic Collapse

The AI Gold Rush: How to Profit from the AI Revolution

Bastet's Shadow: The Hidden Power of Feline Magick

The Bastet Codex: Unlocking the Goddess's Magickal Secrets

Purring Spells: Harnessing Bastet's Healing Frequencies

Bastet's Nine Lives: Rebirth, Transformation, and Immortality Spells

Primal Currents: Hydrocephalus Magick in the Path of Dino Wicca

The Digital Gold Rush: Mastering E-Commerce and Online Sales

Future Shock: Adapting to the Next Decade of Change

The Quantum Mindset: Think Like a Billionaire

Sacred Motherhood: Awakening the Divine Feminine Within

The Mother's Spellbook: Enchantments for Love, Protection, and Prosperity

The Witch's Guide to Parenting: Raising Empowered and Intuitive Children

The Magick of Motherhood: Reclaiming Your Power Through Rituals
The Pagan Path to Self-Love: A Goddess's Guide to Worth and Confidence
Wild Woman Magick: Unleashing Your Primal Power
The Money Magnet Blueprint: Unlocking Unlimited Wealth
Biohacking 101: Unlock Your Body's Full Potential
The Wild Father: A Pagan Guide to Strength and Wisdom
The Sacred Masculine: Unlocking Your Inner Power
The Druid's Compass
The Warrior's Mindset
The Father's Fire
Odin's Path
Ancestral Bonds
The House That Whispers
The Magician's Code
The Wild Hunt
The Green Man's Path
The Altar of Success
The Shadow and the Sword
The High Priestess's Guide to Energy Healing
The Lunar Mother
The Sacred Self-Care Grimoire
The Womb Wisdom Codex
The Wheel of the Mother
The Witch's Guide to Manifestation
The Q2 Reset
The Ultimate Guide to AI-Powered Passive Income
Escape the 9-5
AI Feline Fortunes
The Tear-Stained Grimoire
Razorblade Runes
Cemetery Sirens

The Midnight Wristwatch
The Town That Forgets
AI Horror & Creepypasta
The Hollow Frequency
The Breach Echo
The Quiet Between Worlds
The Sigil of Tharan-Khul
Summon the Vault of Y'ha'ten
The Becoming Codex
The Profit of Az'ra-nar
The Drowned Logos
Echoes of the Eldritch Will
The Deep Ledger
Necronomicon of Networth
Covenant of the Wealthwyrm
The Whisperer's Manifesto
The Rites of Azh-K'luth
The Ark of the Crawling Coin
The Tithe of Shadows
Inkheart Abyss
The Timewinds of Y'ha-nthlei
The Spiral Labyrinth of Azag-Nirrh
The Gallifreyan Heresy of the Black Pharaoh
The Psalms of Nyog-Sotha
Black Rain Alchemy
The Infinite Maw
The Entropic Blueprint
The Oracle of Sh'guul
The Book of Breach
The Drowned Saint's Testament
Dreamcraft of the Sleeper God
The Silence Market
Cthonomics: The Dark Wealth Algorithm

Invocation of the Ten-Eyed King
Wealthbound to the Wyrm Below
Become the Unnameable
Codex of the Sovereign Flame
Rituals of Relentless Becoming
The Shadow Ascends
The Eyes Beneath You
The Will That Wakes Worlds
Silence Is a Weapon
The Mirror That Screams
The Whisper Between Moments
The Mind That Devours Fear
The Myth of the Finished Self
The Architect of Your Madness
The Voice You've Buried
The Discipline of Madness
Stormborn: Awakening Your Inner Tempest
The Mind That Ate Time
Unbind Your Becoming
The Pact You Owe Yourself
The Devourer's Diet
The Acid That Carves the Path
The Tower You Must Burn
The Breath Between Worlds
Speak Like the Deep
The Labyrinth Within
The Spine of the Sea God
Rejection Is a Portal
The Crown You Refused
The Scar Is the Spell
The Lightless Flame
The Habit of Becoming Horrific
ChickenJockey Chaos

The Gatekeeper Within
You Are Not Your Name
The Compass of the Mad
The Archive of Unsent Letters
What the Mirror Can't Show You
The Knife You Needed
Worship Nothing, Become Everything
The Other Voice
The Body the World Forgot
The Vein of the Void
The Black Bone Codex
The Puzzle of the Hidden Self (Millennium Puzzle)
The Eye That Sees the Lie *(Millennium Eye)*
The Ring of Return (Millennium Ring)
The Rod of Relentless Will ***(Millennium Rod)***
The Tally of the Soul (Millennium Tauk/Necklace)
The Key to the Locked Timeline (Millennium Key)
The Scale of Sacred Decisions (Millennium Scales)
Inferno Bites: The UnOfficial Minecraft Lava Cookbook
Rot in the Attic
Prana: The Hidden Force of Your Infinite Self
The Shadow Realm Within: Transforming Darkness Into Destiny
The Borderland Collapse
Claws of Protection: Bastet's Defensive Magick
Mr. Ring-a-Ding's Madness
Yugioh Astrology: Celestial Deckcraft and Duel Destiny (2026–2027 Edition)
The Seal You Signed: Unlocking the Power You Once Feared
The Puzzle of Infinite Minds: Unlocking the Mentalism Hidden Within
The Eye That Mirrors the All: Secrets of Inner Reflection
Doctor Who: The Toymaker's Broadcast

Rootwake: The Carbon Covenant
Skitter Logic: Unlearning the Fear That Built You
Doctor Who: The World That Froths
Rootwake: The Fizz That Rewrites Flesh
Rootwake: Frothfather of the World
The Holly Pact: Blood Beneath the Mistletoe
The 2nd Mass Principle: Building Unbreakable Tribes
Web of Wits: A Survival Guide to Encounters with Anasi the Spider (Aunt Nancy)
The Hexbreaking Handbook: Effective Spells to Remove Curses
Pop Alchemy: Transform Your Life One Sip at a Time
The Mason Code: Leading in Unleadable Times
Petosiris and the Fifth Chamber of Thoth
The Ether Seed Within
The Parent of Tomorrow
Petosiris's Pyramid of Perpetual Wealth
Unlearn the World
Grimoire of the Hollow Tongue
Zodiac Weeds: Finding Your Strain Through the Stars
Aquarius Rises in the Bank
The Sugar God's Smile
The Skinclock Reversal: Biohacking the Face of Time
Debtburn: How to Obliterate What You Owe Forever
The Ice Cream Oracle: What Your Cone Says About Your Future
Silence Is Sovereignty: The Power of Being Unreadable
The Wind That Whispers Through Stone
Path of the Four Directions
Doctor Who: The Maestro's Symphony of Endings
Oxygen Grail: Breathing to Undo the Clock
Zodiacal Collapse: When Stars Devour Time
Teachings from the Red Sand Silence

Doctor Who: Omega – The Broken Equation
Memory Wipe Your Past: Start Over Like a MiB
Mitochondria Prime: Ignite the Core of Youth
A Nest of Roaches
Grub from the Galaxy: MiB Recipes You'll Never Forget
Whiskers of Power: Bastet's Guide to Inner Sovereignty
The Gift Must Cost Them: Negotiation Through Unequal Exchange
The Worm Guys' Wealth Code: Hustle Like an Alien
Bug Out: The Edgar Method for Ruthless Goal Setting
Weaving Life with Spiderwoman's Pattern
Doctor Who: The Rani's Renaissance
How to Get a Job (If You're a Puppygirl)
Speak Through Others: The Art of Proxy Power
T-Rex Your Trauma: Reclaim the Power of Your Primal Self
The Black Briefcase: How MiB Stay Wealthy in Silence
The Thirst Beyond Reason: Understanding Diabetes Insipidus From the Inside Out
Backwoods Witchcraft for Billionaires: The Pagan Path from Dirt Roads to Gold Roads
The Moonshine Grimoire: Fermented Spells for Abundance
The Nameless Geometry
The Wraith's Mixtape: Spellcasting with Songs of Sorrow
The Gallifreyan Gentleman: Silent Wealth, Sonic Confidence, and the Doctor's Code of Living
Sugar Water Confidence
Dino Totems: Spirit Guides from Earth's First Gods
Pumpkin Sigils & Ritual Smoke
The Hózhó Compass
The Distortus Discipline – Order from Inner Mutation
Witchcraft for the Cold-Blooded Soul
Moonlight Over the Blessingway
Water, Interrupted: When the Body Forgets How to Hold On

Deformed but Divine: Embracing Your Asymmetry
Hexes in the Henhouse: The Farm Witch's Guide to Power
The Reversed Flame: A Grimoire of Inverted Power
Salt, Cells, and Sanity: Reclaiming Balance with Diabetes Insipidus
King of the Broken: Crowning the Flawed Self
Moonlight Scars: Emo Moon Magick and the Art of Lunar Sorrow
Noose Spells: Magick of the Hanging Rope
The Goth Cathedral: Rituals of the Broken and Beautiful
The Cretaceous Codex: Dino Spirits and Fossil Magick
The Turkey Bones Ritual
Nine Lives of Manifestation: Unlocking Bastet's Reality Codes
Chaos Muscles: Building Strength from Twisted Pain
Emo Blood Magick: The Veins of Power
The 3AM Flood: Nighttime Urination, Sleep Loss, and the DI Spiral
The Silence Between the Stars
The Lemon Method: Sour Your Way to Success
Starlit Sovereign
The Rite of Twelve Gates: Walking the Gates of the Duat.
Cornbread and Conjure: Recipes for Riches and Rootwork
The Black Rose Rituals: Emo Love Spells and Obsession Magick
The Eternal Goodbye: Death Magick and Rebirth Rituals
Sinkrot: The Drain That Remembers
The Hybrid Mindset: Thinking Beyond Evolution
Bone Dry: Navigating Dehydration Before It Breaks You
Wreathcraft: Winter Sigils and Yuletide Spells
The Rite of Twelve Mouths
S'mores of the Damned: Haunted Recipes for Halloween Night

Rethink the Drink: A Beverage Survival Guide for DI Warriors

The Shadow Chord: Guitar Magick and Sonic

Malformed Yet Majestic: Leading When You Feel Wrong Inside

The Cursed Diary: Ink-Stained Spells of the Emo Soul

Anxiety Off Switch: Emergency Reset for a Fried Nervous System

The Energy Heist: How to Take Back Your Life from Drainers

Beyond the Bathroom: Rebuilding Your Social Life With DI

Coyote's Gift for Decision Makers

Ghoul-Goo: Spooky S'mores You'll Die For

Echoes in the Mirror: Scrying and Self-Destruction Magick

Thread and Thorn: Stitching Spells from Rural Cloth

The Mogwai Mind: Building Untouchable Wealth from Small Ideas

Be Your Own Guide: Trust Your Inner Compass

Hormones in Chaos: The Endocrine Puzzle of Diabetes Insipidus

ChronoCleanse: Detox Your Biological Timeline

The Limb You Hide Is the One That Saves You

Leaves, Bones, and Whisper Spells

The Dinosaur Mindset: Prehistoric Tactics for Modern Wealth

Clawing Back Control: A Bastet Method for Boundaries and Empowerment

Samhain Codes of the Forgotten

Orange Alchemy: The Autumnal Spellbook

Monster Within, Master Without

The Sigil That Sleeps

Hearthcraft: Yule Hearth Sigils and Winter Warmth Spells

Temple of the Purring Moon: Rituals from Bastet's Lineage

When the Earth Remembers Your Footsteps

Food for Mood: Eat to Heal Depression, Not Just Survive It
Witch of the Kudzu Vine: Southern Pagan Wealth Secrets
The Invisible Diagnosis: Advocating for Yourself With DI
The Coffin's Lullaby: Sleep Magick and Nightmares as Portals
Ashes of the Will: Rituals for Erasing the Self
The Fracture Rite: Shattering the Magickal Core
Funeral Candles: The Art of Emo Flame Magick
The Black Grimoire: A Blank Ritual for Writing in Absence
Phantom Thirst: A Halloween Survival Guide for Diabetes Insipidus
The Hollow Crown: Emo Royalty and Magick of the Outcast King
Sandpainting for the Soul
Falling Into Balance: Using the Extra Hour to Recalibrate Life
100 Southern Superstitions That Still Work
The DI Child: A Parent's Guide to Raising Hydrated, Happy Kids
The Jungle of Shame: Escaping the Hidden Lab of Doubt
The Witch's Toast: S'mores Spells and Creepy Confections
The Hoodoo Pantry: Spells from the Mason Jar
The Immortal Fortune: Secret Wealth Lessons from Captain Jack Harkness
The Specter's Embrace: Magick for Channeling Ghostly Lovers
Grateful Waters: A Thanksgiving Survival Guide for Diabetes Insipidus
The Seizure Gospel
Harvestbind: Autumn Sigils and Samhain Spells
Doctor Who: The Algorithmic Awakening
Silent Nights, Steady Waters: A Christmas Survival Guide for Diabetes Insipidus
The Extra Hour Effect: How One Hour Can Transform Everything

Blade Between the Breaths
Running with the Mountain Shadows
Echoes of the Failed Experiment – Becoming a Living Legacy
Swamp Witches & River Ghosts: Real Southern Hauntings
Cornbread Prophecies: Magical Recipes from a Southern Table
Doctor Who: The Signal in the Star
Bloomcraft: Spring Sigils and Equinox Enchantments
Vanisher: How to Disappear from the Internet Without Losing Your Life
The Ultimate Christmas Cookie Cookbook
The Unbreakable Parent: How to Mentally Survive Raising Kids in a Broken World
Time Debt: How to Reclaim the Hours You Didn't Know You Lost
One Month, One Million: Unconventional Cash Creation Tactics
Doctor Who: The Cyber Conversion Protocol
Black Friday Frenzy: The Art of Finding Hidden Online Deals
The Grimoire Buried Under the Apple Tree
Digital Couponing Masterclass: Your Step-by-Step Guide to Black Friday Savings
The Fire Inside the Flint
Shadows on the Ceiling: The Emo Guide to Astral Magick
The Bone-Eaters Beneath Us
Black Friday Bundle Blueprint: Creating Irresistible Product Packages for Maximum Sales
Thirteen Nights of Unbinding
Doctor Who: Engines of Influence
Pumpkin Spice Alchemy: Recipes of Fire and Frost
When Raptor Met Rexy: Prehistoric Lessons in Wild Romance
Oblivion's Candle: Burn the Path Behind You

Campfire Curses and Chocolate: A Halloween S'mores Grimoire
The Wallet That Wasn't Mine: Breaking Free from Inherited Scarcity
The Cola Zodiac: What Your Fizz Says About Your Fate
Frostfire Fortune: Unlocking Winter's Hidden Prosperity
Signal Jamming: Detox Your Brain from Info Overload
The Dust of the Forgotten Rite
The Golden Cat Sigils: Drawing Power in Bastet's Name
Mud Magick: The Prosperity of Getting Dirty
Savory Spicefall: Beyond the Pumpkin Pie
Pumpkin Spice Apothecary Kitchen
The Pumpkin Spice Economy: Turning Trends into Billions
The Ember Veil: 13 Nights of Fire Magick
Financial Freeze: When Earning Triggers Panic
The Gingerbread Alchemist: Sweet Recipes with a Twist
Biosynth Power: Programming Yourself from Scratch
Echoes from the Talking Circle
Truffle Alchemy: Fungus of Fortune
Spores of Power: The Truffle Witch's Handbook
Doctor Who: The Tower That Speaks
The Mycelium Veil: Truffle Magick Unbound
Broke But Ashamed: Healing the Shame Wound of Debt
The Evergreen Mind: Growth Through Winter Stillness
The Black Veil Truffle Rite
The Voice Beneath Symbols
Witchlight on the Bayou: Swamp Spells for Sovereignty
I Grew Up Poor and Now I Sabotage My Success
The Lantern of Hollow Souls
Shutdown Survival: A Citizen's Guide to Thriving When Government Stops
When Abundance Feels Like a Threat: Healing the Hidden Fears of Enough

The Scarecrow Grimoire

Owls of the October Veil

Candlewax and Curses: A Halloween Spellbook

Excavating the Inner Fossil – Transforming Fossilized Thoughtforms into Tools of Power

The Yule Witch's Spellbook: Magick for the Holiday Season

Haunted Christmas: Ghost Stories for Winter Nights

The Christmas Survival Guide: Thriving Through the Chaos

The Bone Orchard Rites

Haunted Commerce: The Ghost in the Marketplace

When Money Triggers the Inner Child

Silent Night with the Silence: A Christmas Thriller

The Lightning Crown: Living and Leading Through Seizures

TARDIS Tidings: Festive Stories from the Whoniverse

Autumn Reset: Slowing Down Without Falling Behind

The Trillion Dollar Soul: Rewriting the Currency of Reality

Truffle Eclipse Magick

Micro-Manifestations: Quick Magick That Works

5-Minute Rituals for Busy Witches

The Marshmallow Massacre: Halloween Treats with a Sinister Twist

Blood and Blackberry Thorns

Magickal Mornings: Rituals for a Blessed Christmas Day

Embers of the All-Hallows Fire

The Pumpkin Market Collapse

The Hour You Gained: Transforming Time Into Power

The Chamber Must Be Sealed: Mastering the Power of Controlled Access

The Cursed Manuscript of Petosiris

The Festive Hearth: Creating Holiday Traditions

Darkness Rising: Thriving as Nights Grow Longer

Harvesting Time: Turning the Year's End Into Your New Beginning

Petosiris and the 13th Zodiac Key

Wagewound: When Paychecks Become Identity Prisons

Walls That Watch

The Silent Feast: Rituals of Power in the Longest Night

The Distortus Legacy : Becoming a Deformed King in a Perfect World

The Hollow Masks

The Gratitude Furnace: Forging Gold from Thanks

Feast of Inner Gold: Eating for Energy and Enlightenment

Haunted Commerce: The Season of Spending Spirits

Fear Bonds: How Panic Creates Profit

Black Friday E-Commerce Playbook: Sales Tactics to Skyrocket Your Holiday Revenue

Budgeting for Black Friday: A Holiday Savings Planner

Haunting the Harvest Moon

The Warrior's Water: Emergency Preparedness for People With DI

The First Sip of the Year: A New Year's Survival Guide for Diabetes Insipidus

Doctor Who: The Thirteenth Node

The Unseen Struggle: Mental Health, Anxiety, and Chronic Thirst

The Hearth's Hidden Ledger: Counting Energies as Currency

The Gift Alchemist: Turning Any Offering Into Gold

The Papyrus of the Bound Spirit

The Magick of Leftovers: Transmutation in the Fridge

Frost and Fortune: Christmas Wealthcraft for the Modern Magus

Last-Minute Gifts: Creative Ideas on a Budget

10 Secrets to Surviving Holiday Crowds

The Witch's Dow Jones

The Witches' Graveyard Shift

Pumpkin Sigils: Carving Rites for Midnight Power

The Secret Shopper's Black Friday Guide: How to Get Early Access and VIP Deals

Fever in the Foundation

The Neuralyzer Reset: Reprogram Your Morning Routine

Lightning Lessons of the White Painted Woman

The Enchanted Snowflake

The Magic Sip: Surviving Disney Parks with Diabetes Insipidus

The One Who Draws Through You

Santa's Secrets: A Magical Holiday Planner

Silent Bells, Loud Miracles: Self-Help for the Season of Stillness

The Sugar Spell Codex: Confectionary Magick of Christmas

Autumn Hexcraft: Fallen Leaves, Fallen Barriers

Sleep Like a Fortress: Build a Life Where Insomnia Can't Survive

Nowhere Was Ever Home

Christmas Under the Stars: A Celestial Holiday Guide

Rentproof: How to Never Be Evicted Again

Get Some Tarot cards: https://www.makeplayingcards.com/sell/apophis-occult-shop

Get some shirts: https://www.bonfire.com/store/apophis-shirt-emporium/

<u>Instagrams:</u>
@apophis_enterprises,
@apophisbookemporium,
@apophisscardshop
Twitter: @apophisenterpr1
Tiktok:@apophisenterprise
Youtube: @sg1fan23477
Hive: @sg1fan23477
CheeLee: @SG1fan23477

Podcast: Apophis Chat Zone: https://open.spotify.com/show/5zXbrCLEV2xzCp8ybrfHsk?si=fb4d4fdbdce44dec

Newsletter: https://apophiss-newsletter-27c897.beehiiv.com/

If you want to support me or see posts of other projects that I have come over to: **buymeacoffee.com/mpetchinskg**

I post there daily several times a day

Get your Dinowicca or Christmas themed digital products, especially Santa Raptor songs and other musics. Here: **https://sg1fan23477.gumroad.com**

Apophis Yuletide Digital has not only digital Christmas items, but it will have all things with Dinowicca as well as other Digital products.

www.ingramcontent.com/pod-product-compliance
Lightning Source LLC
LaVergne TN
LVHW022226200926
848481LV00006B/2143
* 9 7 9 8 3 3 0 5 2 1 4 3 2 *